Educating for Democracy

In our world of unceasing turmoil, an educated citizenry is the first and strongest line of defence for democratic renewal. *Educating for Democracy* shows how students can prepare for the responsibilities of "the most important office in a democracy" – that of a citizen. Education can provide students with the dispositions and skills needed to exercise their role judiciously and responsibly, as a patriot who cares about democracy and as a custodian who cares for democracy. These two aspects of caring call for curriculum-wide reform. The outcome of this reform is a patriot who serves as custodian of democratic culture, where commitment and competence, heart and mind, love and intellect are brought together for the sake of democratic renewal. While nations, as both instruments and proximal objects of care, have an important role to play in this renewal, the ultimate aim is the care and cultivation of a democratic culture.

WALTER FEINBERG is Professor Emeritus at the University of Illinois, at Champaign/Urbana. He is a recipient of the Lifetime Achievement Award from the John Dewey Society and is known for his work on democracy and education. He has served as president of the Philosophy of Education Society and the American Educational Studies Association.

Educating for Democracy

WALTER FEINBERG
University of Illinois, at Champaign/Urbana

Shaftesbury Road, Cambridge CB2 8EA, United Kingdom

One Liberty Plaza, 20th Floor, New York, NY 10006, USA

477 Williamstown Road, Port Melbourne, VIC 3207, Australia

314–321, 3rd Floor, Plot 3, Splendor Forum, Jasola District Centre,
New Delhi – 110025, India

103 Penang Road, #05–06/07, Visioncrest Commercial, Singapore 238467

Cambridge University Press is part of Cambridge University Press & Assessment,
a department of the University of Cambridge.

We share the University's mission to contribute to society through the pursuit of
education, learning and research at the highest international levels of excellence.

www.cambridge.org
Information on this title: www.cambridge.org/9781009219273

DOI: 10.1017/9781009219297

First published 2023

A catalogue record for this publication is available from the British Library.

Library of Congress Cataloging-in-Publication Data
Names: Feinberg, Walter, 1937– author.
Title: Educating for democracy / Walter Feinberg, University of Illinois.
Description: First Edition. | New York : Cambridge University Press, 2023. |
   Includes bibliographical references and index.
Identifiers: LCCN 2022051439 (print) | LCCN 2022051440 (ebook) |
   ISBN 9781009219273 (Hardback) | ISBN 9781009219280 (Paperback) |
   ISBN 9781009219297 (epub)
Subjects: LCSH: Citizenship–Study and teaching. | Democracy.
Classification: LCC LC1091 .F44 2023 (print) | LCC LC1091 (ebook) |
   DDC 370.11/5–dc23/eng/20221110
LC record available at https://lccn.loc.gov/2022051439
LC ebook record available at https://lccn.loc.gov/2022051440

ISBN 978-1-009-21927-3 Hardback
ISBN 978-1-009-21928-0 Paperback

To my great-grandson, Emmet Teoman Capraz. May he have the wisdom and will to help fix this broken world.

Contents

Acknowledgments

My appreciation to Kurt Stemhagen, Catherine Henney, and Richard Franz for their helpful comments on the chapter on math education and for steering me to useful sources on math education and the philosophy of math. My discussions with Stacey Robinson on art and with my grandson Austin Fouss-Feinberg on music were especially valuable as I developed the chapter on the expressive curriculum. Special thanks especially to Dan Brudney and Belden Fields for their very thoughtful critical comments throughout the process of writing the book. Eric Bredo has been my sounding board on a number of my books, including this one. His willingness to read different drafts and his insightful critical comments gently delivered have been both encouraging and invaluable. Thanks as well to Rebecca Bigelow and to the editors at Cambridge University Press for their very careful editorial aid.

This book has been a long time in coming. I began to think about the issues as a student in philosophy at Boston University in the late 1950s and early 1960s. John Lavely and Richard Millard, my undergraduate honors advisors, opened up the world of philosophy to me. Marx Warsofsky, my primary dissertation advisor, introduced me to the world of critical inquiry, while Kenneth Benne, my secondary advisor, helped me to see that there is an intimate connection between democracy and education. I am grateful for their insight and humanity.

Introduction

O, yes,
I say it plain,
America never was America to me,
And yet I swear this oath –
America will be!

Langston Hughes, "Let America Be America Again"[1]

Where climate change, a global pandemic, and the continuing specter of nuclear annihilation threaten life on the planet; where the reality of that threat is denied by special interests, and where that denial is amplified by media hype and rumor mongering; where QAnon-deluded partisans reject the results of a legitimate election and sound science; and where a significant minority of people believe that wearing a medical mask to stem a pandemic is a violation of *their* individual freedom, in such a world, an informed and educated citizenry is the first and perhaps only line of defense. *Educating for Democracy* shows what that defense might look like.

CITIZENSHIP AND THE NEED FOR EDUCATIONAL RENEWAL

Educating for Democracy provides a vision for educational renewal that aims to prepare rising citizens for the responsibilities of democratic participation. This vision is designed to fulfill the idea that "the most important office in a democracy is citizen."[2] I argue that citizenship education should provide students with the dispositions and

---

[1] Poetry Foundation; available at www.poetryfoundation.org/poems/147907/let-america-be-america-again.
[2] Barack Obama, Speech given at McCormick Place, Chicago, January 18, 2017.

skills needed to exercise that office judiciously and responsibly as both patriots who care *about* democracy and custodians who care *for* democracy. These two aspects of caring call for curriculum-wide reform – from the arts and the humanities to the sciences and math. The outcome of this reform is a new kind of *patriot, one* who serves as a custodian of democracy, such that commitment and competence, heart and mind, love and intellect are brought together for the sake of democratic practice and moral renewal. While *nations,* as both instruments and proximal objects of care, have an important role to play in this renewal, the ultimate aim is the care and cultivation of a *democratic* culture.

Recent books on democratic educational reform separate the civic side of education from the academic side. Some focus on science, technology, engineering, and math instruction (STEM), arguing that these hold the key to equal opportunity and good jobs. But equal opportunity and good jobs alone do not make a democracy. Other books focus on civics, defined as a basic understanding of the workings of political institutions. But democracy is more than politics and requires more than knowledge of political practices and institutions. The separation of civics from STEM courses insinuates that civic competence can be separated from technical competence. I argue otherwise: The character of technical competence has much to do with the quality of civic competence, and, conversely, the character of civic competence has much to do with the quality of technical competence.

Educating for Democracy belongs to the long tradition that connects the condition of democracy to the quality of education. This tradition includes classical works by Jane Addams, John Dewey, W. E. B. Du Bois, Thomas Jefferson, Horace Mann, as well as more recent works by Danielle Allen, Kwame Anthony Appiah, Sophie Haroutunian-Gordon, Amy Gutmann, Eammon Callan, Meira Levinson, Stephen Macedo, Marth Nussbaum, Sigal Ben-Porath, and Yael Tamir. Still, the connection between education and democracy extends well beyond the literature in philosophy of education and is interwoven with institutions, such as community libraries, public schools, community colleges, and land-grant universities. This tradition is summed up by an inscription on the Boston Public Library in Copley Square: "The Commonwealth Requires the Education of the People as the Safeguard of Order and Liberty."

THE NEW PATRIOTISM VERSUS NATIONALISM

My idea of the *new* patriot is aspirational. Drawing on Morris Janowitz's conception of patriotism as a self-critical, enlightened civic consciousness appropriate to a highly interdependent world,[3] I use the term *new* as a modifier of patriot to counter the kind of exclusionary patriotic expression that followed the bombing of World Trade Center on September 11, 2001, and is most recently voiced in the xenophobic rhetoric used to deride those refugees seeking safety and asylum. The new patriotism draws on shared feelings and resources to promote a mutual quest for a common good, but it also emphasizes the intellectual side of patriotism, an *enlightened* civic consciousness. It is to be distinguished from nationalism, where the interests of one's own country are advanced exclusively, and where the aim is to establish dominance over others. The new patriotism is not concerned with dominating but rather with the quality of cultural, political, and planetary life, and, with the role democracy, can serve in furthering it.

DEMOCRATIC CULTURE EVOLVES

Democratic culture evolves as a result of new knowledge, innovative technology, visions of emerging possibilities, and fresh challenges and opportunities. Education must prepare rising citizens to both recognize these changes and, where possible, to shape them according to democratic ideals. At first these changes may appear to require only minor adjustments in individual habits, when they actually may foreshadow major transformations in human relationships and social

---

[3] Morris Janowitz, *The Reconstruction of Patriotism: Education for Civic Consciousness* (Chicago: University of Chicago Press, 1983).

norms. Take, for example, *Ms.*, a title that today is largely accepted as an appropriate way to introduce a woman. The title was initially disturbing to many people – women as well as men – not necessarily because they sensed that it signaled the profound changes in gender relations that were on the horizon. Rather, many complained because they felt the term was grammatically awkward and pretentious. In a short time, that simple two-letter title would become tied to rapidly changing reproductive technology and new gender relationships expanding expectations and opportunities for women. These included more women in the workplace and the demand for more opportunity for women in sports and in the professions. As the title Ms. became more acceptable, a new vocabulary emerged with it, serving to label moral, conceptual, and legal innovations. These included such terms as a "glass ceiling," "sexual harassment," and "marital rape."

I realize that the concept of patriotism is problematic for some, often associated with the jingoism that Samuel Johnson labeled the last refuge of the scoundrel,[4] and that demagogues like Joe McCarthy and Donald Trump appropriate to promote their own ambitions. This image of patriotism associates it with the use of irrational anger and fear to harness collective behavior for repressive goals. John Dewey captures the real motives behind this kind of patriotism when, in rejecting the Lowell report and its justification of the execution of Sacco and Vanzetti in 1927, he wrote:

> The rabies that exultantly sent Sacco and Vanzetti to death is proof of how deeply such patriotism may cancer. It extends not only to foreign nations as such, but to foreigners in our own country who manifest anything but the most uncritical "loyalty" to our institutions. Thousands upon thousands of the most respectable elements in the community believed they were exhibiting

---

[4] The Political Views of Samuel Johnson (online); available at https://en.wikipedia .org/wiki/Political_views_of_Samuel_Johnson#:~:text=On%20the%20evening% 20of%207,the%20patriot%20minister)%20and%20his.

patriotism to the nation or to Massachusetts when they urged the death of men who were guilty of the ... crime of being aliens.[5]

In contrast, the new patriot seeks social cohesion through an informed understanding of basic democratic ideas and the knowledge required to advance them. New patriots learn that they are a part of this evolving process and have a responsibility to harness the forces driving it in the direction of the advancement of the growth and development of democratic principles.

Cultivating custodians of democracy requires a deep understanding of the environmental and cultural forces that impel change, as well as the skills to respond to unexpected events in ways that promote inclusive participation. While civics, history, and social studies have traditionally been assigned the task of citizenship education, I will argue that if democracy is to flourish, the education of the new patriot will require the reconstruction of the STEM and expressive (aesthetic) curricula as well. The aim is to create a body of citizens who are committed to maintaining a democratic culture, who are open to change, and can reassess their individual and collective responses to it. Thus, *Educating for Democracy* holds that today democracy requires a new form of patriotism, one where loyalty and commitment are informed by disciplined inquiry and broad participation. This book shows how different subject areas can contribute to this aim.

SOCIAL COHESION AND INDIVIDUAL FREEDOM

Both old and new patriotism aim at social cohesion, but they differ in the way that cohesion is to be achieved and how it is manifested. The old patriotism seeks cohesion through an idealized, unreflective version of the American experience. New patriotism seeks it through openness about privilege and reflection about the possibility for new and expanded forms of equality and solidarity. The old patriotism

---

[5] John Dewey, "The Fruits of Nationalism," *World Tomorrow* 10 (1927), 455.

speaks to the heart – love; the new patriotism speaks to the mind as well – intellect. Democratic practice rests on love and candor, and like the love for one's family, both as individuals and as a caring unit, the new patriotism is an everyday affair. The new patriot is more the custodian than the cheerleader.

If the new patriotic education is to avoid being co-opted by narrow chauvinistic nationalism or rejected as state-sponsored brainwashing, it is critical that patriotic commitment be developed through honest and open representations of a country's history. While age considerations are relevant in determining when certain uncomfortable topics should be presented to students, the history of racism or other distasteful chapters of American history are not to be negated or obscured for the sake of surface social cohesion. Thus, *Educating for Democracy* does not minimize the risk to cohesion that a truthful representation presents, but it does reject the assumption that a candid representation of uncomfortable truths must inevitably weaken a commitment to democratic social cohesion. It shows how a deeper representation, one that embraces the value of dissent, can serve to advance rich, democratic, social cohesion.

While nationalistic chauvinism is inconsistent with the ideals of a democratic education and should be rejected, rising citizens must learn that the rights that protect their own personal freedom depend on their willingness to nurture and sustain a culture that supports and extends those rights to others as well. Thus, *Educating for Democracy* promotes the formation of a body of citizens whose members give others the benefit of the doubt regarding a commitment to democracy, who believe that openness and inquiry are critical for it to thrive, who understand that democratic politics requires a democratic culture, and who have the competencies required to promote it through joint inquiry, civil discourse, and cooperative engagement.

New patriotism requires that action be guided by both reflection and judgment: Reflection is the capacity to distance oneself from familiar cultural patterns in order to address systematic impediments to the realization of democratic norms. Judgment involves the capacity to recognize complexity, to assess the forces that impinge on democracy in a postindustrial age, and to be aware that unintended negative side effects can result from well-intended acts. It involves a capacity to apply general principles to specific conditions as a way to advance a desirable result, and it also involves sensitivity to the consequences of specific commitments to assess the merits of existing interpretations of general principles. The new patriotism entails commitment shaped through reflection and judgment and it involves a willingness to treat present conclusions provisionally and subject to future revision. It requires not only a renewal of the often-neglected lessons about governing traditionally taught in high school civics classes, but it also requires a capacity to evaluate present practices in light of new facts and evolving possibilities and limit. The development of this capacity will require a curriculum-wide commitment to promote the skills and dispositions that healthy democracies require to evolve.

BRIEF SUMMARY OF CHAPTERS

A number of the chapters begin with a description of an ordinary event, some of which I experienced. They are intended to provide perspective. These include such diverse experiences as a discussion with inmates in a local correctional institution about the meaning of freedom; a description of an unsuccessful attempt by philosophers in the former Yugoslavia to create a coherent national narrative; a discussion of how to teach students to divide a fraction by a fraction; and a description of the difficulty of intentionally walking out of step to the drumbeat of a marching band. I use these events to introduce the topic of the chapter, by providing perspective, and to illustrate how a democratic culture is dependent on the everyday habits and acts of ordinary citizens.

Chapter 1: Citizen, the Most Important Office in a Democracy

All *democratic* education is directed against tyranny, but some kinds of tyranny are easier to identify than others. One kind of tyranny involves a visible dictator who controls public and private lives toward arbitrarily determined ends. Another kind of tyranny, more insidious than the first, controls what people come to want for themselves and for others – this is the result of the tyranny of habit. We want what we are conditioned to want, and we often find it hard to imagine anything else. One of the aims of an education for the office of citizen is to provide students with the intellectual tools and to develop the character dispositions required to recognize, monitor, and respond to the tyranny of habit. The remainder of the chapters in the book is an elaboration on this aim and the way it sets the stage for the education of the new patriots and their role as custodians of democracy.

Chapter 2: Educating for the Office of Citizen

Democratic ideas and habits do not arise automatically; they have taken centuries to develop, and stitching democracy together after its fault lines have been exposed, as they recently have been in the United States, is a long-term affair. Citizenship education requires contributions from an extended curriculum – math and science, art, and the humanities, as well as social studies and civics – focused on the specific needs of rising citizens. One place to begin is by taking the idea of citizenship as an office seriously and then asking what kind of education is needed to make that office effective in advancing democratic culture.

Chapter 3: Reflection as an Educational Aim of the New Patriot

The material for this chapter is drawn in part from a class I taught on American pragmatism at a local correctional institution. William, one of the students in the class, asked in response to a reading by the philosopher C. S. Peirce, "Given Peirce's ideas about habit and belief, how could a slave ever develop a vision of freedom if everything around him was designed to make him think of himself as a slave?" In other words, since a habit is something we take for granted, how could we even begin to recognize our own habits as supporting tyrannical relationships? A response to this question and to the role that formal education could play in promoting this recognition is the topic for the remaining chapters in the book.

Chapter 4: The Humanities: Habits of Commitment / Habits of Reflection

One common definition of the humanities is the "cultivation of what is most human in man [sic]."[6] Putting aside the definition's sexism and its Platonic resonance, the humanities involve the stories we tell ourselves about ourselves. Sometimes these stories are about our own personal experiences, as in therapy; sometimes they are about our collective experiences as a people, as in history; and sometimes they are about possible selves, as in literature and philosophy. When we can no longer see ourselves in these stories, cohesion is threatened, and things begin to fall apart. When this happens to individuals, it is seen as a personality disorder. When it occurs in a society, it is seen as a social disorder, and it can be a prelude to social breakdown.

In this chapter, I use my experience in the former Yugoslavia to explore the tension that arises when a national story is challenged and social cohesion breaks down. I then draw a connection between the situation then in former Yugoslavia and the challenges faced by the United States today. The remaining chapters in the book discuss ways in which education can address those challenges and the kinds of knowledge needed to do so.

Chapter 5: The Humanities: Interpretation, Judgment, and the Evolution of National Narratives

This chapter addresses the tension between truth and social cohesion. Since all stories are an interpretation of some event or behavior, the examined life is always an interpretation of an interpretation. But the interpretation of one's own national history is not of some distant object: It is of the self, and it has a purpose – to open up and explore the

---

[6] R. S. Crane, *The Idea of the Humanities* (Chicago: University of Chicago Press, 1967), vol. I, p. 21.

possibilities that the past offers in the present for the future. This chapter examines the qualities of a good interpretation and role of the humanities in shaping it. I show how progress in interpretation is possible and argue for a dialogical view of interpretation where meanings evolve as contexts change, as new knowledge becomes available, and as the implications of different possible interpretations become clearer.

Chapters 6 and 7: Science, Technology, Engineering, and Math (STEM)

Mathematics and science present two challenges for democracy. The first is to promote equal opportunity. Mathematics is a major factor in the selection of candidates for advanced education and for rewarding professions. One task for custodians is to support fair selection procedures, ones where present performance is relevant to future responsibilities, and where irrelevant factors like parental income or background or excessive and unnecessary requirements do not intrude on selection. The second challenge is to nurture specific qualities of democratic culture and thought that can promote democratic social cooperation and reasonable levels of social cohesion. A great deal of recent educational reform has focused on the first of these challenges to the neglect of the second. The next two chapters show why this neglect is a mistake, and explores the connection between math and science education and democracy.

Chapter 6: STEM and the Democratic Aims of Mathematics Education

This chapter explores the potential of mathematics education for the formation of critical democratic habits of open-mindedness, flexibility, and concern for meaning. It shows how different approaches to the teaching of math serve to model different conceptions of authority and analyzes the implications that these conceptions have for democratic engagement.

Chapter 7: STEM and the Democratic Aims of Science Education

The very integrity of the scientific process depends on preserving the institutional framework that is critical for maintaining and reproducing the methods and attitudes required for systematic inquiry. A major aim of science education for custodians of democracy should be the development of the habits and skills required to protect the institutional production, application, and dissemination of reliable knowledge. Custodians need to understand how science is informed by values at virtually every stage, from the problem selected for study to the way a problem is defined and supported, to the methods chosen to test a scientific claim, to the logic that moves the argument from premise to conclusion, and from conclusion to recommendations for policy and action. This requirement is important for citizens in general and for citizens who work in scientific fields in particular.

Chapter 8: The Expressive Curriculum

The term "expressive curriculum" is meant to include not only formal canonical works in the art and music curriculum but also public monuments, like the Vietnam Memorial, and public rituals such as pledging allegiance to the flag. In addition to their aesthetic function, many of the works in the expressive curriculum are also intended to advance a cohesive picture of a virtuous nation and to promote fidelity to it. In this chapter I explore the question why the expressive curriculum matters and what is at stake in the way it is developed and expressed. I argue that custodians of democracy have the responsibility to assure that cohesion is not bought at the expense of truth and to find ways to align them. In other words, the task of the custodian is to shape new patriots so that they demand truth as well as cohesion.

Chapter 9: Democratic Education and Moral Growth

Democratic citizenship education requires an evolutionary conception of morality as dynamic, open to deliberation and changeable in response to new knowledge and altered conditions. In order to meet the challenges of a changing physical and social environment, the new patriot requires an education that promotes the idea of moral progress and innovation. In this chapter, I offer a modified evolutionary view of

the possibility of moral progress and its implications for democracy
and for the education of the new patriot.

A Final Note on Social Cohesion

One of the definitions of social cohesion is the emotional qualities that
enable members of a group to stick together. This definition can encom-
pass many different kinds of emotions from the triumph felt through the
beat of a marching band, to the fear of a dictator, to the loyalty and
friendship of a military platoon, to the commonality of purpose and
shared grievance of workers on strike, to the frenzy of a mob.

Democratic cohesion differs from all of these in its mutual
commitment to free expression and individual growth within the
context of an ever-evolving society. People in a democracy are held
together as a cohesive unit by a sense that interdependence is a
condition for growth, self-expression, and personal independence.
This idea was expressed by John Dewey when he defined democratic
faith as "faith in the continuing disclosure of truth through directed
cooperative human endeavor."[7] The result of directed *cooperation* is
not only a better understanding; it is also a self-transformation of both
the individual and their communities.

Because democracy is a special kind of moral practice, one that
aims to enhance the development and growth of all, it promotes a
certain kind of social cohesion – one that is best described as horizontal rather than hierarchical and as cultural rather than just political.
Not a marching band but a jazz ensemble where "'personal identity
comes into focus ... in the complex of attitudes that constitutes the
individual's sense of orientation' of one's location in relation to others
and the circumstances they share."[8]

[7] John Dewey, *A Common Faith* (New Haven: Yale University Press, 1934/1962),
p. 26.
[8] Gregory Clark, quoting Kenneth Burke, *Civic Jazz: American Music and Kenneth
Burke on the Art of Getting Along* (Chicago: University of Chicago Press, 2015),
p. 16.

I   Citizen, the Most Important Office in a Democracy

Citizenship is the single most important office in a democracy. Like the office of the crown in a monarchy, it both legitimizes and symbolizes all other offices. And just as the office of crown requires a special kind of education, one suited to the highest office of a monarchy, so too does the office of citizen require a special form of education, one suited to the highest office in a democracy. While the education required for the future citizen is vastly different from that required for the future monarch, it is in each case essentially a moral enterprise as well as a political one. It is concerned with the well-being of others, and with the goodness of the institutions, and laws that support it.

Yet, while the educational needs of monarchs are often carefully attended to, the educational needs of citizens are too often taken for granted and developed haphazardly, or confused with vocational education, narrowly defined. True, students may be taught about the political mechanisms of democracy in a civics class, but this lesson will barely scratch the surface of the knowledge needed to exercise their office. Custodians of democracy need to go deeper. They need to do more than internalize a body of facts and procedures. They need to understand the deeper principles and dispositions that underlie legitimate change. But the expression of these principles evolves over time. Learning how to occupy the office of citizen requires a capacity to continuously evaluate present practices in light of new facts and evolving democratic ideas.

Take the question of respect – a basic and universal right. Yet respectful conduct is a specific learned skill, performed differently at different times and in different places. "Children should be seen and not heard" was once a common formula for the way a child should show respect to an adult, but it is not common practice any longer. Forms of respect change over time, sometimes as a result of great struggle. Consider the following implicit rules: Do not address a woman as "girl," unless you are a close friend! Avoid the appellations *Miss* or *Mrs.*; when introducing her to colleagues, use *Ms*. Even though the rules for these innovations are not hard to state, those caught in the midst of a generational shift often have great difficulty conforming to them. Much the same is happening today around issues of gender fluidity.

Those who inadvertently fail the test of "political correctness" may be likened to children who have been told to mind their manners but who have no idea what they have done wrong. In fact, learning how to be *properly* politically correct may be more difficult than the child learning to "mind her manners." In the latter, something new has to be learned, while in the former, before the new behavior can be learned, the old behavior has to be abandoned – but we do tend to trip over our old habits. If we are fortunate, much of this surface learning will be picked up haphazardly, without a formal curriculum or a plan of study. However, history will not stand still, and proactive citizens need to understand more than just how to follow existing rules because these will change. They also need to grasp the principles behind the rules and find ways to inform others, without appearing to be condescending or patronizing. And they need to learn how to recognize and discuss evolving cultural innovations. This calls for a deep understanding of the historical and philosophical aspects of evolving values and dispositions and the institutional practices that reflect them.

ELEMENTS OF CULTURAL DEMOCRACY

Cultural democracy involves a self-conscious vision of a community evolving toward greater participation and openness. It is cultural because it relies on a set of widely shared practices, meanings, and expectations. It is democratic because the rights and liberties of one individual are supported by the rights and liberties of all. Consider an early example from George Washington in his striking letter to the Hebrew Congregation in Newport, Rhode Island.[1]

Gentlemen.

While I receive, with much satisfaction, your Address replete with expressions of affection and esteem; I rejoice in the opportunity of assuring you, that I shall always retain a grateful remembrance of the cordial welcome I experienced in my visit to Newport, from all classes of Citizens.

The reflection on the days of difficulty and danger which are past is rendered the more sweet, from a consciousness that they are succeeded by days of uncommon prosperity and security. If we have wisdom to make the best use of the advantages with which we are now favored, we cannot fail, under the just administration of a good Government, to become a great and a happy people.

The Citizens of the United States of America have a right to applaud themselves for having given to mankind examples of an enlarged and liberal policy: a policy worthy of imitation. All possess alike liberty of conscience and immunities of citizenship. It is now no more that toleration is spoken of, as if it was by the indulgence of one class of people, that another enjoyed the exercise of their inherent natural rights. For happily the Government of the United States, which gives to bigotry no sanction, to persecution no assistance requires only that they who live under its protection should demean themselves as good citizens, in giving it on all occasions their effectual support.

It would be inconsistent with the frankness of my character not to avow that I am pleased with your favorable opinion of my Administration, and fervent wishes for my felicity. May the Children of the Stock of Abraham, who dwell in this land, continue

---

[1] From George Washington to the Hebrew Congregation in Newport, Rhode Island, August 18, 1790 (online); available at https://founders.archives.gov/documents/ Washington/05-06-0200135.

to merit and enjoy the good will of the other Inhabitants; while everyone shall sit in safety under his own vine and figtree, and there shall be none to make him afraid. May the father of all mercies scatter light and not darkness in our paths, and make us all in our several vocations useful here, and in his own due time and way everlastingly happy.

George Washington.

When Washington wrote, "while everyone shall sit in safety under his own vine and figtree," he was affirming a right of all citizens to thrive within their own communities. This was considerably different from the universal rights as defined by the French Revolution, where citizenship rights were bought at the cost of public religious expression. And then when he wrote, "May the Children of the Stock of Abraham, who dwell in this land, continue to merit and *enjoy the good will* of the other Inhabitants," he was speaking broadly of a cultural democracy sustained more by *habit* than by law where one of the principles of this democratic culture was respect for individuals *within* their associations as well as outside of them.

THE HISTORY OF THE OFFICE OF CITIZEN

The origin of the word *citizenship* is entailed in the very meaning of democracy, which derives from *demos* (Greek for "people") and *kratos* (Greek for "rule"). Combining the two, one has the idea of government "based on the will of the people, and that ultimately political power should lie with the people as a whole."[2] Obviously democracy did not arise all at once out of the head of Greek political and military figures like Cleisthenes and Pericles, but the social practices they inspired continue to incite demands for greater participation.

---

[2] Derek Heater, *A Brief History of Citizenship* (Edinburgh: Edinburgh University Press, 2004), p. 23.

TOWARD A MORE PERFECT UNION

The aim, imbedded in the Constitution, of a "more perfect union" would seem like a contradiction, paring the absolute term *perfect* with the comparative, *more*. The grammatical purist will object that something is either perfect or it is not. It cannot be "more perfect." However, the phrase "more perfect" is not a grammatical mistake. It is an affirmation of the possibility for moral evolution and moral growth. As such, it is a rejection of both moral absolutism on the one side and moral relativism on the other.

Absolutists view the moral law as *never* changing. An act is always either right or wrong. However, absolutists fail to account for the fact that new knowledge and changing conditions challenge settled moral principles opening them up to revisions and fresh interpretations. Certainly, "thou shalt not kill" has the ring of an absolute, but how shall we define "killing" in light of modern knowledge and technology, like scanning a brain and not finding any activity? Shall we define removing life support from a person pronounced as brain-dead as killing? What about assisting the suicide of a person known to be terminally ill and in grave pain and distress?

In contrast to absolutism, relativism holds that the moral landscape is *ever* changing, and what we count as moral is *only* a temporary human-made construction. The problem here is with the simple word *only*. True, morality is human made – but the word *only* seems to minimize the making. All advances in morality are human made, but this does not mean that all claims to morality are equal. To note that something is *only* human made should signal that it is subject to critical evaluation and improvement.

Hence where some relativists seem to dismiss moral ideas as *only* human constructs, I want to cheer and say yes and hooray for whoever did the constructing, assuming they did it well and for a good end. We cannot be indifferent about the *process* of this construction or its appropriateness when addressing a problematic situation. To see something as a human construct is only the beginning of wisdom.

The next step is to appraise that construction as fit for a given purpose. A house is a human construct, but certainly some houses are better constructed than others.

Democracy, though, is more than a human construct; it is a continuing process of culture-constructing where the makers themselves constitute the object being made. As agents of *a more perfect union, custodians* are an intrinsic part of that evolution. I use the metaphor "cultivating," borrowed from gardening, to describe the process whereby those who attend to constructing of "a more perfect union" are at the same time transformed into more democratic citizens.

There is a distinction between being a citizen *in* a democracy and being a *democratic citizen*. The one describes a standing, the other describes an office. To be a citizen in a democracy is to be entitled to all the rights of citizenship. To be a *democratic* citizen is to take on responsibility for shaping a culture that supports those rights for all. It calls for an education where *appropriate* democratic values are infused into every subject from math and science to the arts, humanities, and vocational areas, and across disciplinary boundaries into the ethos of the school and the relations between teacher and students, students and students, and teachers and administrators.

CITIZEN: A MIDDLE POSITION

Citizens occupy a middle position in an evolutionary process. They draw on resources and ideas developed by past generations, and they use those resources and ideas to address present and future concerns. Constrained by a past they can only partly grasp, they are obligated to a future they may never completely experience. The resources include some experiences and ideas, institutions, and technologies that are readily available, such as inherited histories, ideas about justice, procedures for resolving conflicts, and government institutions. They also include resources not so *readily* available and that may need to be excavated, such as stories of the marginalized groups, repressed visions, lost opportunities. But constrained as they are, from the point of view of the present, the past will always appear somewhat strange, and the future will always be somewhat obscured. The past gives us resources to use in the present in order to affect the future, but our understanding of the past and future both get changed in the process.

The entirety of citizenship education, from the sciences to the arts and humanities, is to be undertaken with this middle position in mind, with a humility toward a partially understood past and an openness toward a future yet to unfold. Here loyalty is owed to the ideas and institutions that make this unfolding susceptible to human agency. And an education for citizenship requires a rigorous program that begins at home, is shaped through school, and is advanced in the workplace – a program that aims at insight, precision, and application.

Education for rising citizens, a term I use to indicate young people who are in the process of learning to occupy the office of citizen, must stitch together past and future, balancing a sensitive understanding of a less-than-ideal past with the critical spirit required to shape a "more perfect" future. An education for citizenship then involves both a comprehensive reconstruction of the past conditions, through which present understandings are shaped, and a critical awareness of possibilities these conditions served to obscure. It is an education into both context and consequences, informed by an awareness of the limitations of our own understanding and by a general but partial understanding of the consequences of individual and collective action. The education of the *democratic* citizen is aimed at character – at refining feelings, deepening and expanding cognition, and promoting thoughtful action.

2   Educating for the Office of Citizen

I know of no safe depository of the ultimate powers of society but the people themselves.

Thomas Jefferson, *Letters*

Citizenship is also a collective responsibility. It's not just individual and family, but also that we have a stake in each other's future ... especially in a time where it is so fractured.

Our Common Purpose[1]

In a democracy, the highest office is the office of citizen.

Supreme Court Justice Felix Frankfurter

There is no advantage in the best of laws, even when they are sanctioned by general civic consent, if citizens themselves have not been attuned, by the force of habit and the influence of teaching, to the right constitutional temper.

Aristotle, *The Politics*

INTRODUCTION

Alice is a seventy-five-year-old woman living in Maine. It is winter, and the temperature has dropped to zero degrees. Her husband is about to turn up the heat when she offers him a heavy sweater and puts one on herself.

There is nothing especially heroic about this act. It will not be written up in the local paper nor be reported on in the evening news.

---

[1] Commission on the Practice of Democratic Citizenship, Allen, Heintz, and Liu (chairs), *Our Common Purpose: Reinventing American Citizenship for the 21st Century* (Cambridge, MA: American Academy of Arts and Sciences, 2020).

Yet Alice, concerned about global warming, is doing everything she can to reduce her carbon footprint, from putting solar panels on her home to buying an electric car, to curtailing travel, to turning down the heat. And while there is no law forcing her to do so, nor is she paid for doing "the right thing," she is acting as if she were commissioned to protect the planet from global warming.

Without being consciously aware of it, by setting examples for others, Alice is acting as a custodian of democracy. She is acting voluntarily to address an important social need. There is no law that says, "Do not turn up the heat!" or "Put on a sweater!" But her actions serve to communicate the kind of implicit rules that need to be followed to address an oncoming crisis. In this book, I suggest ways in which education can serve to cultivate people like Alice, and in doing so produce a new kind of patriot: the person who quietly loves her country for what it can be and who takes quiet steps to care for it.

DEMOCRACY AS CULTURE

Democracy is not just a set of political practices protecting individual rights expressed through majority rule, although it is that. It is also a set of cultural ideas and values reflected in appreciation, thought, behavior, and institutions, and developed through education.

"Speak truth to power!" may be a familiar cliché, but it is also a basic democratic right that requires cultural protection. John Stuart Mill, one of the originators of liberalism, held that free speech was a condition not only for individual expression but also for social advancement.[2] By "social advancement," he meant the same thing as the founders of this country meant when they called for "a more perfect union." Societies, as well as individuals, can grow and develop, and their best ideas about moral development can still be improved.

Speaking truth to power implies more than a *right* to speak. It also entails an education where competence in seeking and recognizing truth is critical, and where those in power are willing and able to

---

[2] John Stuart Mill, *On Liberty* (New York: New American Library, 1962), pp. 184–204.

listen. *Rising citizens*, the term I use to identify students as future custodians of democracy, not only need to develop the dispositions that civic participation requires, but they also need to develop the skills to do so intelligently.[3] As a rights-bearing individual, a citizen has legal protection against arbitrary action by the state and state officials. As a custodian of democracy, the citizen is the ultimate authority for defining, implementing, and protecting those rights, and extending them to others.

This conception of citizen, as more than a rights-bearing individual but as both a custodian who cares for those rights and as a patriot who protects them, goes back to the Greek and Roman idea of the dual role of citizen as a member of society who both rules and is ruled. This was expressed by the Athenian general, Pericles, in his description of the Athenian citizen.

> Here each individual is interested not only in his own affair but in the affairs of the state as well: even those who are mostly occupied with their own business are extremely well-informed on general politics – this is a peculiarity of ours: we do not say that a man who takes no interest in politics is a man who minds his own business; we say he has no business at all. We Athenians, in our own persons, take our decisions on policy or submit them to proper discussion: for we do not think there is an incompatibility between words and deeds.[4]

Granted, citizenship in Athens was restricted to a few Athenian males – excluding women, slaves, and foreigners – nevertheless, Pericles' idea of the active engaged citizen is still an idea worth educating for. As Leonardo Bruni wrote in praising the democratic qualities of Florence in 1428: "When a free people are offered the possibility of attaining offices, it is wonderful how effectively it

---

[3] Derek Heater, *A Brief History of Citizenship* (Edinburgh: Edinburgh University Press, 2004), p. 2.
[4] Quoted in ibid., p. 25.

stimulates the talents of the citizens."[5] Or, as Justice Frankfurter declared, "In a democracy, the highest office is the office of citizen." However, other than a few courses in civics – courses too often neglected – the educational requirement for the office of citizen has not received much national attention.

School reformers too often mistake the goal of economic mobility for that of active, democratic citizenship. Consider that one of the most prominent educational reformers, E. D. Hirsch Jr., advanced the significance of historical figures, like Washington, Jefferson, and Lincoln, not for their ideas about democracy, but rather their instrumental value as cultural capital – by which he meant economic capital.[6]

If, however, we take seriously Frankfurter's assertion that citizen is an office in a democracy, we need to also take seriously the kind of education needed to exercise that office. My argument is that such an education cannot be confined to one or two courses, civics or social studies, but rather it must be infused throughout the curriculum, in math and science as well as the arts and humanities.

LEARNING TO BE DEMOCRATIC

In simplest terms, "culture" refers to those shared meanings, collective expectations, and practices that facilitate human communication, decision-making, and action.[7] Culture functions, much like language, to reshape our original sounds and movements – our babbles and flailing, words and gestures – into something coherent and recognizable by others as meaningful.

Learning to become a *democratic* citizen is something like learning a second language. If you have doubts, watch a couple of

---

[5] Quoted in ibid., p. 56.
[6] E. D. Hirsh Jr., *Cultural Literacy: What Every American Needs to Know* (Boston: Houghton Mifflin & Co., 1987).
[7] For a more detailed treatment of this concept, see my book, *What Is a Public Education, and Why We Need It: A Philosophical Inquiry into Self-Development, Cultural Commitment and Public Engagement* (Lanham: Lexington Books, 2016).

two-year-old toddlers grapple over a toy. Sharing, a quality of a democratic culture, is learned, as are habits of inclusion, taking turns, fairness, and waiting in line. Just as it is easier to learn to speak one's mother tongue than a second language, so too it takes less effort to include and care for people who look like you and are part of your family or intimate circle of friends than it is to engage with people who are different from you. "Birds of a feather flock together" because it is simply a lot easier to converse with and relate to those who share your language and experience.

Because democratic culture rides alongside of other, more spontaneous cultural expressions, its practices, and the reasons for them, often need to be learned. Why can't I treat my boss to dinner if I want to? Why can't the professor date his student? Why can't the official take money for a special favor? What is wrong with the film director offering the actress the role in exchange for sexual favors? The answer to all of these questions involves a deep understanding of the regulation of power and basic ideas about fairness that serve as part of the definition of a democracy. In democracies, in particular, one has to learn to differentiate between one's private and one's public rights, responsibilities, and interests. Learning to differentiate between your private and public selves can be difficult.

Citizens serve as *custodians* of a democracy when they go beyond claiming their own individual rights and consciously work to shape a culture that enhances the independence and flourishing of all. The two words, *independence* and *flourishing*, are both critical. Some societies – think of the Confucian cultures – want their members to flourish, but they reject the possibility that the flourishing could ever take place independent of well-defined, thick social relations and interlocking loyalties, such as child to parent, mother to father, father to leader. Some others – think of the ideology of the rugged individual – promote the ideal of independence, but they reject the idea that anyone should be responsible for someone else's flourishing. Advancing these dual goals of independence and flourishing, and doing so intentionally, is critical if a democratic culture is to grow and be maintained.

Democracy requires the development of certain skills and dispositions. Part of the democratic education of young children involves teaching them to monitor some of their own initial feelings, say of repugnance about another person, whether it be directed toward unfamiliar food, dress, race, or religious beliefs. The educator Vivian Paley devoted her delightful and wise book *You Can't Say You Can't Play*[8] to helping children control this impulse.

Moreover, as Eric Weber puts it, "people" along with a commitment to "promoting an environment in which each person can develop a sense of ... self respect" and "develop their own interests and capacities"[9] are critical features of democracy. This kind of impulse control has practical as well as moral value. It is a condition for easy cooperation of individuals from different backgrounds, enabling them to work together, and it sets the stage for leadership to be dispersed among different individuals, depending on their talent, not on their birth.

CULTURE COMES FIRST, POLITICS SECOND

Citizens as custodians of a democracy take on the responsibility to protect, maintain, and, when necessary, reconstruct the cultural conditions required to keep a democracy going and growing. While preparation for the political responsibilities of citizen – voting, serving on juries, serving as civil servants and office holders – is critical, preparation for cultural responsibility is equally important but less frequently acknowledged.

A democratic culture is reproduced from moment to moment in the way we treat and respect one another in day-to-day interaction. Cultural democracy underscores the importance of reason and

---

[8] Vivian Paley, *You Can't Say You Can't Play* (Cambridge: Harvard University Press, 1993).
[9] Eric Thomas Weber, "Converging on Culture: Rorty, Rawls and Dewey on Culture's Role in Justice," in *Essays in the Philosophy of Humanism* (online); available at www.academia.edu/11931633/Converging_on_Culture_Rorty_Rawls_and_Dewey_on_Cultures_Role_in_Justice.

influence rather than coercion and power, evidence rather than dogma, equality rather than hegemony, and participation rather than domination. A democratic culture provides legitimacy to democratic institutions, including the institutions of politics, by shaping the capacity to distinguish between legitimate and illegitimate expressions of power. An education for the office of citizen requires the development of certain ways of perceiving and thinking (habits of mind), engaging with others (habits of relationships), and expressing moral dispositions (habits of feeling) that traditional subjects like science, math, and the humanities, among others, can serve to develop.

Citizens as *cultural* officers of democracy differ from *political* and *legal* officers in that they have no special, legal status. Of course they can also occupy political and legal offices, but as cultural officers, their role is to promote the habits that democratic systems require to maintain civic engagement. Their authority is strictly moral and educational. Unlike political custodians, they can only influence. They cannot coerce. And their influence must conform to democratic standards of transparency and truth telling. Weber, again echoing Dewey, puts it well:

> The term "culture" ... brings with it a sense of community or of presence within an environment, as well as the kind of feeling that implies inseparability of the self from the wider whole. Culture, furthermore, refers to a set of conditions – pre-cognitive as well as post – which envelop persons in sets of needs, practices, tools, and habits.... In other words, persons in a culture or in an environment are thereby part of that culture or environment, affecting it even as they are in turn affected as well.[10]

Moreover, as Dewey saw, culture is the deeper side of democracy. Politics, as important as it is, depends on a wider cultural understanding.

---

[10] Weber, "Converging on Culture," p. 237.

> Our original democratic ideas must apply culturally as well as
> politically … If we cannot produce a democratic culture, one
> growing natively out of our institutions, our democracy will be a
> failure. There is no question, not even that of bread and clothing,
> more important than this question of the possibility of executing
> our democratic ideals directly in the cultural life of the county.[11]

Culture is foundational when it is constituted by mutually recognized, communally reinforced expectations and shared meanings that
facilitate social cohesion across generations. Democratic culture promotes coherence across primary cultural units and social groups.

DEMOCRATIC SOCIAL COHESION

Democratic pluralism requires what Aristotle called "political friendship"[12] among individuals within, as well as across, groups. The idea
of political friendship describes an extended community of fellow
feeling, and it highlights the voluntary features of political relationships. It is the quality that allows a society to hold together without
dictators, or demagogues, and absent unnecessary coercion or the
excesses of chauvinistic patriotism. Of course there are other factors
as well, such as what Melissa Williams calls a shared fate.[13] Our
common fear of climate change, for example, provides a collective
incentive to cooperate, but political friendship suggests a more
enduring quality.

In a democracy that encourages political friendship among individuals who have different group affiliations, social cohesion is a mark
of the society's goodness. This kind of social cohesion is different from

---

[11] John Dewey, *Politics and Culture*, 1932, p. 238, as quoted by Weber, "Converging
on Culture," p. 257.

[12] Aristotle, *The Politics of Aristotle*, Ernest Barker, tr. (Oxford: The Clarendon Press,
1957).

[13] Melissa Williams, "Citizenship as Identity, Citizenship as Shared Fate, and the
Functions of Multicultural Education," in Kevin McDonough and Walter Feinberg,
eds., *Citizenship and Education in Liberal-Democratic Societies* (Oxford: Oxford
University Press, 2003), pp. 208–247.

traditional patriotism, where emotional allegiance is directed vertically from individual members of different groups to the nation as a whole. Here allegiance is directed horizontally, as well as across cultural differences. It is often fostered by the arts and sports and the development of the capacity to enjoy the achievements of people from many different backgrounds. Here patriotism is a quiet quality that binds plurality into unity as needed.

Social cohesion refers to the extent to which members of a society identify with one another, understand one another, trust one another, and are willing to cooperate with one another.[14] Whether or not social cohesion is good depends on how it is achieved and what ends a cohesive group or community adopts. Ethnic cleansing is often undertaken for the sake of social cohesion, but few would see a socially cohesive, ethnically cleaned society to be a good society. So, while social cohesion is important for any society, for democracies, the way cohesion is achieved and the level of dissention it enables is as important as cohesion itself.

One of the educational aims of modern-day democratic pluralism is the development of horizontal social cohesion, or the connectivity across different groups – ethnic, religious, gender, and ultimately national. *Democratic* social cohesion is different from social cohesion, as commonly understood, in that it is as concerned with the process by which cohesion is formed as it is with the social end state. Democratic cohesion involves not just compliance, but voluntary compliance; not just trust, but informed trust; not just coordinated action, but reasonable and openly arrived at coordinated action, and it requires a capacity to maintain an open democratic, experimental process amidst changing practices and norms. These are the qualities required by *the citizen as a custodian of democracy*.

---

[14] Jan Delhey, Klaus Boehnke, Georgi Dragolov, Zsófia S. Ignácz, Mandi Larsen, Jan Lorenz, and Michael Koch, "Social Cohesion and Its Correlates: A Comparison of Western and Asian Societies," *Comparative Sociology* 17(3–4) (2018), 426–455. DOI: https://doi.org/10.1163/15691330-12341468.

DEMOCRACY AS A MATTER OF HABIT: SOME PERSONAL EXAMPLES

Episode 1

When I was about nine or ten years old, I was walking aimlessly on a sidewalk in my neighborhood, and I almost ran into a middle-aged woman walking in the opposite direction. To avoid a collision, I moved to my right, just as she moved to her left, and then as a corrective action, I moved to my left just as she moved to her right. After one more unsuccessful try at passing, she ordered me to stand still so she could pass on my right, which she did while asking rhetorically whether my parents had not taught me that I was supposed to stand still to let a person pass. I was not sure just what rule she had in mind, and I was unclear about what the rule meant. Was it that males were to allow females to pass? Or was it that the younger people should allow older people to pass? Whatever rule she was thinking of, I was pretty sure I had not been taught it. Nevertheless, even though I was unsure about the rule, I followed her directive, and ever since, I have tried to make it a habit to stand still whenever a similar occasion arises. This avoids many collisions except on that rare occasion when the other person has been taught to follow the same rule – although I have never met such a person that I know of.

Episode 2

As a college student in the 1950s, I was always expected to open the car door for my date. I would stop the car at the curb, she would sit demurely while I got out, and I would hustle across the front of the car to open her door. When I did, she would slowly emerge. It never occurred to me, nor I think to her, that she was perfectly capable of opening her own door and must have done so whenever she drove by herself. But whatever her skill as a driver, whenever we were together, she expected me to be a "gentleman," as defined by the times, and I always tried to oblige.

Episode 3

In the early 1970s, as the women's movement was just beginning to pick up steam, I was walking into the University of Illinois Library with a female colleague when we approached the rather heavy outer door. With my arm stretched out, I stepped in front of her, intending to open it. Upon my action, she demanded to know, "What are you doing!?" When I responded that I was opening the door, she told me in no uncertain terms that she was perfectly capable of opening doors for herself. So I stepped aside as she opened it to let me pass through. She then followed. I am still a bit unclear about the appropriate behavior of door opening, so I watch for subtle cues whenever walking with a woman. Age, position, and status may come into play, but the most acceptable rule seems to be whoever is closest to the door should open it.

My encounter with the woman on the sidewalk initiated the birth of a habit. I still don't know the exact reason why *I* was the one expected to stand still. Was it because I was younger or because I was male? In any event, it still seems like a good idea, and I still try to practice it, as it serves to facilitate cooperative activity, satisfactory to both parties. The woman was able to go her way, and I was able to go mine – albeit feeling a bit chastised. Nevertheless, a more exact rule could have been even more helpful: say, in the case where a man and a woman meet going in opposite directions in the same lane, the man should always stand still to let the woman pass; another possibility: If two men or two women meet in the same lane, the younger should always stand still to let the older person pass. (Of course, that might be awkward and require everyone to carry a birth certificate!) Additional rules could be added; in the case of two men or two women of the same age, for example, the taller should stand while the shorter passes, and so on. Some rule is more efficient than no rule. A rule – like the car coming from the right has the right-of-way – can guide safe action efficiently.

A lot of collective behavior is like this. It is habitual and designed to advance mutual interests more efficiently. But not every act is aimed at mere efficiency. Ceremonial acts, such as saluting the flag, serve to

reconstruct the idea of mutuality, channeling emotions as an acknow-
ledgment that we are all in this together. They function to construct a
sense of togetherness – a community of feeling. Problems arise when
the act is mistaken for the principle that it is designed to represent and
to which a community of feeling is supposed to be attached. The flag is
itself intended to symbolize, among other things, a right to protest,
including a right to protest by burning the flag. To prosecute flag
burning serves to deny the principle of free speech that the protest
represents.[15] Some failures in democracy can be attributed to the
confusion between the act and the principle. Such failure indicates
that a deep conception of democracy may be lacking.[16]

LAW AND POLITICS FOLLOW CULTURAL CHANGE

A custom is a habit that sets expectations and takes on the moral
authority of the group.[17] It may or may not serve to aid efficient action
or mutual desires. From the standpoint of efficiency alone, the dating
behavior I described earlier is an example of an inefficient custom. The
library encounter is an example of an efficient one: Whoever is nearest
to the door should open it. But efficiency was not the only point.

Behind the traditional custom – man opens door for woman –
was a set of assumptions about gender identity and the proper roles of
men and women, assumptions that took time to surface and be challenged. When I was dating, opening the door was to be taken as a sign
of respect and care of the stronger for the weaker, but by the time
I started to teach, it was sometimes being taken as a symbol of
domination and a reinforcement of gender stereotypes. The question
of who was to open the door for whom became an issue of negotiating
between these two meanings: care or domination.

---

[15] *Texas* v. *Johnson* 491 U.S. 397 (1989).
[16] Mark Olssen, *Liberalism, Neoliberalism, Social Democracy: Thin Communitarian
Perspectives on Political Philosophy and Education* (New York: Routledge, 2010),
p. 63.
[17] John Dewey, *Human Nature and Conduct* (Carbondale: Southern Illinois
University Press, 1922/1988), pp. 43–59.

If it had just been a question of opening a door, there likely would have been little at stake. However, the tone of my colleague's voice when she asked, "*What* are *you* doing!?" clearly seemed an accusation: Are you trying to dominate me? This *accusatory tone had been shaped by a long history* where opening the door for "the weaker sex" was a part of a larger social framework that assigned property rights to men while denying them to women. Thus, for a long time, the idea of sexually assaulting or raping one's wife was not only legally but also conceptually impossible because the idea of marital rape was viewed as an oxymoron. A woman belonged to her husband – as the marriage ceremony said, "Do you take this man to love, honor and *obey*." As the "weaker" sex, women had historically been prohibited from taking on rough and tumble fields like law.

For the most part, these deeper meanings were taken for granted, except in the rare case in which they were challenged and brought to the surface, as in the Illinois Supreme Court's denial of Myra Bradwell's right to practice law in Illinois. As a judge of the court wrote in 1873:

> The law has always recognized a wide difference in the respective spheres and destinies of man and woman. The harmony of interests and views that belong to the family institution is repugnant to the idea of a woman adopting a distinct and independent career from her husband.[18]

Historically, a married woman had no independent legal existence and was legally prohibited from making binding contracts without her husband's consent. This played heavily in the Supreme Court of Illinois' decision: "The paramount destiny of women is to fulfill the noble and benign offices of wife and mother."

The contest over the library door was thus a contest over meaning. I saw the move as the polite and customary thing to do – a way to show respect. She took it as an act of domination. I placed it within

[18] *Bradwell* v. *Illinois* C. G. R. Co., 562 F.2d 561.

the grid of etiquettes that included good manners, kindness, and consideration; she placed it in the grid of power, dominance, and subordination. Her objection to my grab for the door was grounded in a larger set of meanings and in a growing awareness of new possibilities for women. It was also a contest over role relations and economic resources, over who should be considered for positions at the university and who should be accepted as legitimate candidates for promotion. To say that she was right is not to say that I was mistaken about my intentions. It is, however, to say that in the larger scheme of things, and given our similar roles at the university, in reaching for the door, I was reinforcing the habits in which men were perceived as strong and women as weak. Whereby as a consequence of their presumed greater physical strength, men were afforded rights that women were denied.

CIVICS AND BEYOND

Formal citizenship education, as taught in civics and social studies classes, is most often about political institutions, formal practices, and landmark historical events. Matters such as who should open the door for whom or whether the man or the woman had the right-of-way when their paths threaten to collide are considered mundane, not weighty enough for serious study. Yet these seemingly *mundane* practices illustrate that democracy, along with our understanding of it, changes with time and circumstance. Their very ordinariness calls for an aspect of citizenship education that will teach students how and why practices change as a result of the reconsideration of the meaning of basic principles and the conditions that lead to new interpretations and practices. This kind of education certainly requires understanding the structure and practice of government, as taught in civics and history courses, but it also marks a deeper purpose where the task of citizenship education is to sensitize students to the deeper meaning of present practices and the conditions that support them. Educating for the office of citizen is more like teaching students to navigate a sailboat toward a dock against the wind than it is like teaching them to drive a car down a straight highway. For the skipper of the sailboat, the near-term destination will change as a result of prevailing conditions, but the long-term intended destination remains the same.

Uncertainty is a feature of democratic life, but there are skills that enable us to maintain the right direction. When cultural meanings clash, as they do in everyday life, it is useful to have citizens who understand the deeper reasons for the change and the clashing interpretive frames that give rise to the differences. This is the task not just of a single subject or of a group of subjects. Nor is it a task that can be accomplished in a single year. Different subjects, like civics and social studies, math and science, religious studies and the arts, have a contribution to make. What we need to keep in mind is the final destination rather than a particular course or grade level.

For the rising citizen, the critical lesson is that democratic societies continually change as a result of changing conditions, emerging possibilities, and new knowledge. The basic principles of democracy summarized in the phrase "all men [sic][19] are created equal," in terms of their moral worth, provides the guideline for determining whether the change is progressive or retrogressive. Progressive change encompasses much more than politics, as critical as that is. Democracy is, as Olssen proclaims, "A *transformational ideal* that can always be improved, or deepened still further."[20] Democracy is a cultural invention, and democratic education is an education into that invention.

Democracy is more than a formal set of rules and related institutions and offices; it is more than the merely prescribed official practices. Democracy depends on understanding when a rule calls for a new interpretation, and democratic education involves developing the kind of disposition that is open to the formation of new interpretations when older ones become dysfunctional.

---

[19] Note how the use of *"sic"* illustrates the point being made.
[20] Olssen, *Liberalism, Neoliberalism, Social Democracy*, p. 81.

3 Reflection as an Educational Aim of the New Patriot

Our stile [*sic*] and manner of thinking have undergone a revolution, more extraordinary than the political revolution of the country. We see with other eyes; we hear with other ears; and think with other thoughts, than those we formerly used. We can look back on our own prejudices, as if they had been the prejudices of other people. We now see and know they were prejudices and nothing else.

Thomas Paine, 1782[1]

It has been frequently remarked that it seems to have been reserved to the people of this country, by their conduct and example, to decide the important question, whether societies of men are really capable ... of establishing good government from reflection and choice or whether they are forever destined to depend for their political constitutions on accident and force.

Alexander Hamilton, *Federalist*, no. 63, p. 341

Each of us has a moral obligation to stand up, speak up and speak out. When you see something that is not right, you must say something. You must do something. Democracy is not a state. It is an act, and each generation must do its part to help build what we called the Beloved Community, a nation and world society at peace with itself.

    While my time here has now come to an end, I want you to know that in the last days and hours of my life you inspired me. You filled me with hope about the next chapter of the great American story when you used your power to make a difference in our society. Millions of people motivated simply by human compassion laid down the burdens of division. Around the country and the world, you set aside race, class, age, language and nationality to demand respect for human dignity.

John Lewis[2]

---

[1] Thomas Paine, "A Letter Addressed to the Abbé Raynal on the Affairs of North America," English translation (London: J. Ridgway, 1795), p. 38.

[2] John Lewis, "Together, You Can Redeem the Soul of Our Nation: Though I Am Gone, I Urge You to Answer the Highest Calling," *The New York Times*, July 30, 2020.

Democracy "has to be constantly discovered, and rediscovered, remade and reorganized."

John Dewey

INTRODUCTION: REFLECTION – THE AIM
OF PATRIOTIC EDUCATION

Recently, I was teaching a course on American pragmatism to a group of inmates at a state prison. The course was part of a program sponsored by the Educational Justice Project based at the College of Education at the University of Illinois. The youngest of my students, William, was twenty-four; the oldest, Mark, was seventy.

The topic of this session was the philosophy of Charles S. Peirce, the founder of American pragmatism. We were discussing Peirce's essay, "The Fixation of Belief," and specifically his doctrine of truth. Peirce argues that our beliefs are not just ideas that we hold in our minds. Rather, beliefs are expressed in everyday habits as the implicit presuppositions of action. For Peirce, belief, not doubt, is our normal state of affairs. When people walk up a flight of stairs, or stand on a balcony, they do so believing that the foundation will hold, just as we all believe that a ball tossed up will fall down to the earth. Peirce defined a belief as a premise one would act upon without doubt or hesitation, like the premise that a familiar balcony will hold you.

For Peirce, doubt is not just an intellectual exercise, as the philosopher Descartes believed. It is physical – the irritation of belief – an actual uncomfortable state caused by a conflict in belief that disrupts action. But this conflict also serves to initiate inquiry. Successful inquiry eliminates doubt, enabling activity to continue. The aim of inquiry then is to eliminate doubt, fix belief, reinstate habit, and resume activity. Truth is an ideal, the term we use for beliefs that hold up in the long run and after subject to systematic inquiry.

The readings sparked a thoughtful discussion. Mark expressed support for Peirce by describing how he had adjusted his beliefs over his fifty years in prison, moving from rebellion to acceptance. By accepting his sentence, Mark was able to accept his situation and take advantage of the experiences the prison offered. He was now an accomplished artist.

William took issue and challenged Peirce's idea of truth, using the experience of slavery as a counter example. He wondered, if doubt only arose when habits were interrupted, and then ended with the resumption of activity, how could slaves ever have imaged themselves as free or rebelled against their condition? If Peirce was correct and the resumption of activity was the end of inquiry, then the slave would never have even been able to imagine the possibility of freedom. In other words, he would have accommodated to the master's conception of him as just another beast of burden. William concluded that the idea of freedom must therefore arise out of more than a concern to reconstruct habitual activity, especially when there is something inherently wrong with that activity.

William was inadvertently addressing the same issue that the philosopher Hegel addressed in his famous "Lordship and Bondage" chapter in his *Phenomenology of Mind*.[3] For Hegel, the slave comes to see himself as *essentially* free – or, in Hegel's terms, as a being who exists in and for itself – by recognizing that the fear that he feels is *his* fear. It does not belong to the master. As he becomes conscious that his fear belongs to him, he realizes that he has an emotional life of his own and that he fears not *for* the master; rather he fears *the* master *for* himself. Fear, and the *consciousness that the fear belongs to me*, is the beginning of wisdom or self-consciousness. Hegel's insight is that the seeds of freedom are planted when a person realizes that their emotional life is their own. Reflection is the name of the process through which consciousness is revealed to itself, allowing it to serve as its own object for development and growth. Reflection is not only necessary for individual growth, but it is also

---

[3] G. W. F. Hegel, *The Phenomenology of Mind*, J. B. Baillie, tr. (London: George Allen & Unwin, 1931), pp. 228–240.

the condition for the growth and evolution of democracy and thus serves as the aim of the education of the new patriot in her role as a custodian of democracy.

REFLECTION AS THE EDUCATIONAL AIM FOR THE NEW PATRIOT

Hegel's account of slavery can be taken as a *thought* experiment designed to expose the connection between reflection and freedom. The slave is not just afraid, as any nonhuman animal might be afraid. He is rather *aware* of his fear, and this awareness tells him that slavery is not a natural state – that freedom is his true destiny and slavery is just a condition that has been imposed by an external, arbitrary source. It is *the awareness* of fear, of his subjective emotional state, that makes the slave *human* and that sets freedom as his ultimate aim. But freedom is more than just a psychological condition of the individual. It is ultimately a cultural condition supported by collective habits and institutions. Collective habits, or cultural practices, shape institutions, and cultural practices can both limit freedom and can provide the conditions for liberation. One of these conditions is the awareness of the fact that the master is himself dependent on the labor of the slave and on the slave's status as an inferior being.

THE OBJECT OF SELF-REFLECTION

The novelist Fyodor Dostoyevsky wrote thus about self-reflection:

> Every man has reminiscences which he would not tell everyone but only his friends. He has other matters in his mind which he would not reveal even to friends, but only to himself, and that in secret. But there are other things which a man is afraid to tell even to himself, and every decent man has a number of such things stored away in his mind.[4]

---

[4] Dostoyevsky, *Notes from Underground.*

Reflection is often uncomfortable because, as Dostoyevsky reminds us, it is only the unpleasant features of the mind – the things that we do not want to reveal even to ourselves – that are the objects of self-reflection.

Consider the friend who consistently places himself at the center of everyone else's story. You are telling him about your recent accident. He interrupts to recount an accident he had in the distant past. Someone praises a colleague's contribution to the project. He retorts that his contribution was more significant. You mention a friend who has recently received a promotion. He complains that he deserved it more. In other words, he places himself at the center of everything. To be forced to look at and acknowledge his own self-centered proclivity would no doubt be painful because it would require the quality to which self-centeredness is blind: self-awareness. As Dostoyevsky understood, self-reflection can be painful, but it is also necessary if we are to identify and change dysfunctional behavior and develop an openness to the possibility of change.

Self-reflection involves exploring dispassionately one's habits and self-image. As Rebecca Goldstein writes:

> This maneuvering outside of oneself is a difficult thing to do, given the terrifically powerful centripetal forces ... keeping one quite literally, together, in the process warping one's worldview, making one's vision of the world conform to one's commitment to oneself. But the dispassionate knowledge of oneself is also, to the extent that we can achieve it, the most self-expansive of all experiences ... One can never inhabit one's own self quite the same way again, which is to say that one has changed.[5]

It would be wrong to think that this maneuvering outside of oneself is strictly a psychological event where a person is able to inspect their own individual thoughts. To some extent it is that, but it also

---

[5] Rebecca Goldstein, *Betraying Spinoza: The Renegade Jew Who Gave Us Modernity* (New York: Random House, 2006), pp. 183–184.

involves seeing one's relationship to others – family, friends, and community – as an object to be examined. The word "alienation" is a strong one, but it accurately describes this situation where a person comes to see the self, at least temporarily, as an alien other.

But it is not simply the isolated self, divorced from all relationships, that is the object of alienation. It is the self in its relations with others and the values that bind them together. Alienation – making an object of oneself in relationship – is the first step toward evaluation, and evaluation is a first step toward a "more perfect" self, including an extended sense of self as citizen.

Alienation is the reason reflection is painful, and it is also the reason it is so often resisted. This is a frequent theme of films, such as a *Price above Rubies* or *Unorthodox*, both about the cost to women who try to separate from the orthodox religious community of their birth and who, through reflection, begin to understand how their communal relations serve to restrict them. It is also the theme of classics like *Romeo and Juliet*.

The psychological cost of alienation is familiar to anyone who has become aware of the dysfunctional dynamics of their own family and the impact it has on their own behavior. In these situations, alienation serves as a middle step between dysfunctional and subconscious responses and newer consciously chosen patterns of behavior. As a way station between an unsatisfying past and an unknown future, between the dynamics of a set of dysfunctional relationships and the more functional dynamics of the emerging set of relationships, alienation has its costs as the familiar becomes strange and its dysfunctionality recognized. The price is not only a changed set of relationships. It is a changed self. In effect, the pain of feeling an inadequate or repulsive self is like the irritation of doubt experienced by a Peircean inquirer.

Alienation is a topic for psychoanalysis when an individual exhibits dysfunctional or self-defeating behavior. A woman has begun to feel distant from her husband and finds a therapist who helps her to give voice to her feelings and analyze them. Here recognizing alienation is a necessary step in addressing pain. Alienation plays a similar role in the education of custodians of a democracy, and as we will see in Chapter 4, it is not always successfully resolved.

Nevertheless, alienation is often unavoidable, and reflection is a critical but painful factor in the development of both individuals and nations. As David Silverman writes:

> Serious, critical history tends to be hard on the living. It challenges us to see distortions embedded in the heroic national origin myths we have been taught since childhood. It takes enemies demonized by previous generations and treats them as worthy of understanding in their particular contexts. Ideological absolutes – civility and savagery, liberty and tyranny, and especially us and them – begin to blur. People from our own society who are not supposed to matter, and whose historical experiences show how the injustices of the past have shaped the injustices of the present, move from the shadows into the light.[6]

This movement from shadow into light is disruptive from the standpoint of national cohesion. It reveals wrongs that continue to fester; it raises questions about the standard tropes upon which national identities have been constructed, and it demands a reckoning.

Reflection is not a one-time thing. It is a set of habits that are developed and can be called upon when a person's identities and commitments conflict. These habits provide needed emotional distance from familiar cultural patterns and allow conflicting demands on loyalties and identities to be addressed. Nationhood requires reasonable levels of social cohesion and assumptions of good faith if differences are to be addressed in a way that the benefits of mutual recognition can be realized. While there are some *political* constants, such as the willingness of defeated candidates for office to accept the election of and be

---

[6] David J. Silverman, *This Land Is Their Land: The Wampanoag Indians, Plymouth Colony, and the Troubled History of Thanksgiving* (New York: Bloomsbury Publishing, 2019), p. 1.

governed by their opponents,[7] the action of the supporters of the
defeated candidate in the 2020 election notwithstanding, the elements
of *cultural* cohesion will differ in different time periods. New cultural
pieces are formed out of older ones, and older ones divide again and
then recombine in new ways. As a result, cohesion is always somewhat
unstable – a work in process, experienced by each of us in unique ways –
but from the vantage point of a specific set of cultural convergences,
such as middle class and white, or Italian background and straight, or
female and Catholic, or professional and Black, and so on. At certain
times one or another element of the convergence achieves priority.
This is what is meant by "intersectionality." At any given time, cultural reflection may call out some set of these cultural configurations.
The call may be sparked by something as *seemingly* inconsequential as
a joke, for example, when a person who inadvertently laughs at a quip
about gays has her own binary sexual identity called out and challenged. Reflection requires a certain level of discomfort if conflicting
relations and loyalties are to be acknowledged and addressed. What
counts as a joke is often more than a question about humor. To call out
a joke as sexist, for example, can reach deep into the moral map of an
individual or an era. Listen to a comedy show from the 1940s and the
connection between humor and moral patterns becomes obvious.

Reflection takes us outside of ourselves, allowing new possibilities to be seen – even leading to changes in the way reality is labeled
and described. Consider the way in which we used to identify a person
with a disability as "crippled," indicating a functioning disorder as an
essential attribute of that individual, and absolving society from
addressing it. Jonathan Glover shows the connection between the
way we think about a disadvantage and our ideas about justice.

> It used to be thought natural or inevitable that disabled people
> could not use certain buildings, trains, and buses. But strong

---

[7] Steven Levitsky and Daniel Ziblatt, *How Democracies Die* (New York: Crown, 2018).

campaigning has made us see that failure to provide disabled access is a choice and that this "passive exclusion" can also be an injustice.[8]

Certainly, it took strong campaigning, but other things were needed as well: technological innovations in the form of elevators, the development of sign language, and then voice recognition software, for example. And it took a considerable change in language and how we talk about difference in terms of "challenges" that are amenable to fixes.

Technological advances, from simple ramps to computerized speech, together with organized protests from communities of people with disabilities, promoted different ways to think about the supposed limitations associated with disabilities. Helpful too was a change in the idea of the cause of a disability, from some kind of individual deficiency to an environmental deficit, from an individual failing to a failure to provide an adequately supportive environment. It is shocking to realize that few city planners prior to the 1970s thought of adding a ramp to a sidewalk. An environmental defect – as opposed to a supposedly individual deficiency – is correctable by an environmental fix, like eyeglasses that can aid nearsighted people, or a landing in the middle of a long staircase that can aid both older people and those with mobility issues.[9]

EDUCATION, ALIENATION, AND THE TYRANNY OF HABITS

All *democratic* education is directed against tyranny, but some kinds of tyranny are easier to identify than others. One kind of tyranny involves a visible dictator who controls public and private lives toward ends set by an autocrat. Another kind of tyranny, more insidious than the first, manipulates through deception, what people come

---

[8] Jonathan Glover, *Choosing Children: Genes, Disability, and Design* (Oxford: Clarendon Press, 2006), p. 60.

[9] Lorella Terzi, *Justice and Equality in Education: A Capabilities Perspective on Disability and Special Educational Needs* (London: Continuum, 2008).

to want for themselves and for others – this is the consequence of the tyranny of habit. We want what we are conditioned to want, and we often find it hard to imagine anything else, even when satisfying those wants is harmful. The campaigns of tobacco companies described in Chapter 7 is a case in point.

Back in the classroom, William's challenge to Peirce involved the recognition that the tyranny of habit can be much harder to address than the tyranny of a visible, malevolent dictator – although slavery certainly involved both. But a first step is to recognize that tyranny for what it is and find ways to distance oneself from it. This requires, as Ringen puts it, an education aimed at illuminating the higher purpose of citizenship, as "a system of collective decision making where the aim is to define a common good through the mechanism by which citizens together hold the ultimate power of control."[10]

An education for the office of citizen is not confined to one or two subjects like civics or social studies. Rather, because the aim is to develop reflective participants capable of cooperative deliberation about the practices that will govern their lives, educating officers of democracy should involve the full range of subjects from math and science to the humanities and the arts. The aim of such an education is to monitor and advance freedom where, as Ringen puts it, "The meaning of freedom is to be in control not only of choice but also of the purpose of choice,"[11] not only for the individual but also for the society as a whole.

> [The idea that] freedom means to be able to do as one wishes is a
> dangerous idea. It is dangerous to the individual because it easily
> encourages the delusion that the quality of freedom can be reduced
> to the quantity of abundance and from there stimulates a life of

---

[10] Stein Ringen, *What Democracy Is For: On Freedom and Moral Government* (Princeton: Princeton University Press, 2007), p. 219.
[11] Ibid., p. 204.

frivolous and futile pursuit of more of everything irrespective of value and purpose. It is dangerous to community because it discourages decency, cooperation, and trust. It is dangerous to the standing of freedom in the world because it is an idea that will for good reasons be seen as perverse against the backdrop of mass poverty, environmental decay and cultural confrontations.[12]

The freedom to be able to do as one wishes leaves one open to the manipulation of those advertisers who have the means to shape and manipulate wishes. The alternative is an education for reflective freedom, where one's immediate desires can be evaluated in terms of both their origins and their consequences. Here one considers not only the intended consequences of a private act but also the side effects on others. These include the institutional constraints needed to control unwanted side effects (e.g. pollution) and to create better synergies (positive side effects), like the effects of early childhood education on others, as well as the children in question.[13] Ringen explains:

> The Awareness of Values and norms must be learned.... The capacity to reason must be learned.... Citizens who have liberty owe it to themselves to acquire the competence to live freely. By so doing they also do their community a service because they are more likely to live in a way that invites cooperation and contributes to a climate of trust.[14]

An education for the office of citizen contributes to that climate of trust by promoting a society where evidence counts, reasonable inter-pretations are welcome, tentative conclusions are tested, and emanci-patory imagination encouraged.

---

[12] Ibid., p. 203.
[13] Appreciation to Eric Bredo for this wording. These themes are developed more fully in John Dewey, *The Public and Its Problems* (Athens, Ohio: Swallow Press, 1927/1954).
[14] Ibid., p. 212.

DEMOCRACY IS AN UNFOLDING: NOT A ONCE AND FOR ALL REVELATION

Democracies grow as the constructed nature of individual and social habits becomes a matter for mindful consideration and are evaluated for their capacity to advance social inclusiveness and individual and collective growth. Danielle Allen describes the process nicely:

> In order for a moral idea to become real in the world, it must trail after it multitudes of concrete actions. The project of reimagining and reinventing the web of habits that bring ideas to life in the world is vast, even infinite.
>
> An idea is weak until people can imagine in concrete terms the specific actions they will take under its ascendency.
>
> New scripts are invented only as people begin to undertake new actions. Spaces must be ripped open in the existing web of human habits, which have a tightly adhesive grip on the human spirit.
>
> Sometime those spaces are ripped open by those who are worst-off under present conditions. Think ... of the slaves who liberated themselves from plantations during the Civil War and forced both North and South to change their policies toward runaway slaves and their military service.
>
> New actions must be attractive in themselves, intuitively, to people's spirits, even without reference to the ideals that give them meaning, in order for people to break through old habits once and for all and adopt new ones.[15]

In other words, people must learn and then relearn to be democratic. To become a custodian of democracy is to recognize its dynamic quality and treat its present manifestation as an object for deliberation and change.

The irritation of doubt arises not just from activity arrested, as Peirce believed, but from a recognition that there are opportunities to

---

[15] Ibid., p. 241.

expand the moral principles of democracy in new ways and to then attach them to new groupings, as William understood. Vision is an interruption of habit. Principles can provide a projection of desirable habits yet to be formed and are essential in extending democracy from one grouping to another.

The word "grouping" is intentional, helping to explain the meaning of the phrase "a more perfect union." One of the signs of a democracy is the developing awareness of people who share a certain characteristic – a grouping – into a *group*, an identity organized around the perception of a shared experience, say, that they are all discriminated against because of that characteristic. Hence, there will always be new claims for liberation that democracies will need to address.

But the newness is not just random. Principles matter! They define what is just and fair and enable the expansion of fair treatment from one group to another. The emergence of modern feminism partly as a response to sexist practices in the Civil Rights and Anti-Vietnam Movements is an example of the usefulness of an appeal to principles to justify the extension of democratic practices to beyond the immediately targeted groups – nicely summed up by the quip, "Put your money where your mouth is."

CULTURAL DEMOCRACY AS A MATTER OF HABIT: CONTINUING WILLIAM'S INTERROGATION OF PEIRCE

The novelist Kazuo Ishiguro, in his *Remains of the Day*, identifies the ability to banter across social roles/class as a critical divide between democratic and aristocratic societies. Stevens, the British butler in the novel, simply can't understand how to respond to his new American boss/master when the master tries to initiate playful bantering. Cultural democracy is manifested in seemingly small things, a tone of voice, a seating arrangement, a greeting, the punch line of a joke, bantering. Political practices are certainly important, but democratic political practices rest on a robust democratic culture, where habits of democracy are informed by deep-seated principles grounded on the ideas of inclusion, participation, and growth.

There is no one script that can be assigned that will make a people democratic, but there are some general ideas that are useful measures of democratic culture. Particular conditions count in determining just what kind of habits are consistent with a democratic culture. As conditions change, so too will our notion of acceptable habits change.

THE COST OF REFLECTION

Reflection enables citizens to identify the behavioral patterns that give rise to breakdowns in relationships so that they can better understand their source and possible remedy. When the object of reflection involves a close connection – say a family, a community, or a country – it may sometimes come at the unhappy cost of alienation, either temporary or permanent. When temporary, we find a way to fix the problem and move on. Permanent alienation results in estrangement – literally turning the friendly and familiar into the strange and the hostile. But continuing alienation is a sign of incomplete reflection, where the ultimate aim is to probe possible avenues for repairing breakdowns. Educating for the office of citizen is preparation for this move.

CONCLUSION: A DISCIPLINED APPROACH
TO CITIZENSHIP EDUCATION

Modern educational reformers have been particularly keen to promote math and science, as well as technology and engineering education. However, reform has primarily emphasized the importance of these fields for vocational advancement and national superiority, with little attention paid to their possible contribution to the education of democratic citizens. In Chapters 4–8, I will reexamine these and other fields and show the unique value that they can play, both individually and together, in forming a new level of democratic citizenship.

4   The Humanities

Habits of Commitment / Habits of Reflection

No country can last long without a shared narrative. You wonder, on an Independence Day when the mood of the country is more angry and fearful than it's been in a long time, if this nation can ever have such a thing again.

Timothy Egan, *The New York Times*, July 3, 2020

The hermeneutic task is to identify, in any interpretation, which preconceptions are productive (ones that further interpretation) and which are nonproductive (ones that perpetuate misunderstanding).

Shaun Gallagher[1]

The humanities are ... the vital core of an education for a democracy; the proof of that statement is furnished daily by democracy's enemies. Dictatorships cannot tolerate the humanities.

Bernard Knox[2]

INTRODUCTION: TWO FUNCTIONS OF THE HUMANITIES

In this chapter and Chapters 6–9, I show how the humanities can be employed in the service of cohesion, without sacrificing a truthful representation of the past, warts and all or their value in their own right. I begin by looking at the case of the former Yugoslavia, where despite an effort by humanists to shape a coherent national and democratic narrative, the country fell apart. I then use the Yugoslav experience to explore a potential role for the humanities today in

---

[1] Shaun Gallagher, *Hermeneutics and Education* (Albany: State University of New York Press, 1992), p. 91.
[2] Bernard Knox, *The Oldest Dead White European Males and Other Reflections on the Classics* (New York: W. W. Norton, 1994), p. 104.

possibly repairing a strained American narrative and the torn identity that it represents. The question at the core of these two chapters is whether the humanities, subjects like history, philosophy, literature, classics and the like, can be used to stitch together different experiences into an acceptable national narrative. The experience of the former Yugoslavia suggests otherwise, but I am somewhat hopeful that given an appropriate understanding of the role humanities can play in helping people understand themselves, that repair is possible. The Yugoslav example is meant as a warning that the construction of a unifying, truthful national narrative is anything but easy, and I draw on my own school experience to show the power and influence of the stories we are told. I also hope to show, for those readers who are skeptical about the influence of any national narrative on a country's future, that we are all imbedded in certain stories that tell us who we are and that help shape our sense of self. The task, as I see it, for the humanities is not to deny their political influence but rather to help different peoples to recognize one another as constituting part of the same national project, while acknowledging their differences. While the situation of the former Yugoslavia and the contemporary United States differ significantly, the Yugoslav example is meant as a warning, exposing the fragility and the importance of national cohesion. It is also meant to raise the profile of the humanities and to suggest ways they can aid truthful democratic formations.

PART I   THE HUMANITIES, NATIONAL COHESION, AND A FAILED NARRATIVE: THE CASE OF YUGOSLAVIA

Two Faces of the Humanities

The humanities have two sides, which for convenience I call the speculative and the interpretive. The speculative sees the humanities, and especially philosophy, as a necessary guide to collective human action;[3]

---

[3] R. S. Crane, *The Idea of the Humanities and Other Essays: Critical and Historical* (Chicago: The University of Chicago Press, 1967), vol. 1, p. 41.

it aims to change the world. Here "any enduring system of human relationships must involve shared conceptions of the good as the basis for social unity."[4] Plato's philosopher king set the model for appropriating philosophy as a guide to collective life, but others like Hegel or Marx add a temporal dimension, viewing history as unfolding toward a more voluntary, more humane, destiny.

The interpretive side views the humanities as a field of studies concerned not with changing the world but with interpreting it. This side is concerned with human understanding, and meaning. Here the aim is to enable many different forms of life to coexist without imposing a single preferred script on any of them. The interpretive dimension emphasizes particularity and multiplicity, not singularity.[5] From the standpoint of the speculative dimension, this is a weakness rendering the interpretive dimension merely academic. On the other hand, from the standpoint of the interpretive side, the speculative dimension is intrusive and insensitive to differences. It is too quick to want to change the world according to whatever master narrative it favors, without consideration for the meaning and richness of any of the real lives that people experience. In the process, complexity is ignored for the sake of some far-off and distant goal.

As a product of constructed imaginations, national identity is fragile, especially in pluralistic democracies where cohesion depends on the faithful execution of an aspirational ideal, such as "the American Creed," a statement about fairness and merit. Cohesion is difficult to build and easily fractured.[6] But I will argue that when fractured, the humanities may provide the material needed to stitch together a new identity, one that emerges out of the old. Repairing

---

[4] Everett K. Wilson, "Introduction" to Emile Durkheim, *Moral Education: A Study in the Theory and Application of the Sociology of Education* (New York: The Free Press, 1973), p. X.

[5] Jean-Francois Lyotard, *The Postmodern Condition: A Report on Knowledge*, Bennington and Massumi, tr. (Minnesota: The University of Minnesota Press, 1979), pp. 27–31.

[6] Benedict Anderson, *Imagined Communities* (London: Verso, 1983), pp. 37–46.

fractures and maintaining a cohesive democratic identity is the work of citizens serving as custodians of democracy. But failure is always a possibility.

The Price of Failure

The price of a failed construction is high, and failure is not infrequent. Consider for example the fate of the former nation of Yugoslavia, a country that was consciously built on a speculative humanistic foundation and that at one time appeared to be a viable social democracy. I first became aware of the Yugoslav situation in 1974. Just as I was about to embark with my wife and children on a sabbatical leave, first to Dubrovnik in Yugoslavia and then to London, I got a request from my former professor at Boston University, Bob Cohen, and from Noam Chomsky at MIT to check in on a Yugoslavian philosopher and dissident, Mihailo Marković. Marković, a leading public intellectual, hero of the resistance during the Second World War, and the most prominent member of the Yugoslav *Praxis* school of philosophy, had not been heard from for months. His friends in the West knew that he and the other members of the Praxis group had been harassed by the political allies of Marshal Tito, the country's leader, and Cohen and Chomsky were concerned about their well-being.

The plan was that I would fly from Dubrovnik, where I was participating in a seminar on peace and conflict resolution, a label that would prove to be sadly ironic, and then take a side trip to Belgrade, where I would meet with Marković. If all were well, I would send a telegraph back to Cohen saying, "Having a great time. Wish you were here." If Marković and his colleagues were in trouble, then the message "Help, Need Money!" would be sent instead.

Marković met me at the airport and expressed concern that his car and house were bugged and that it was dangerous to talk there. So we walked around a drab neighborhood of cinderblock apartment houses for a couple of hours as he filled me in on the details. His passport had been lifted and his classes suspended. I followed up the meeting with the telegram, "Need money." As a result, Chomsky and

Cohen publicized the situation in the *New York Review of Books*,[7] and a few years later, after the Praxis philosophers' condition had worsened and its members had been suspended from teaching, I published a separate article in the *Christian Science Monitor* about their plight.[8]

During my visit, Marković told me he had spent much of his life working to build a national Yugoslav identity, promoting the idea that Yugoslavia was committed to developing a unique form of socialism, where enterprises would be managed by their workers, rather than run by private owners, as in capitalism, or by central authorities, as in Soviet-style communism – socialism with a human face.[9] Marković believed that Yugoslavian socialism could flourish without the murderous excesses of Stalinism or the appalling inequalities of Western capitalism.

The word *praxis* is Greek for theory-guided practice. For Marković and his group, it meant a world where planning and laboring were united in each enterprise through a body of managers elected by and from the workers themselves. The goal was to give everyone a voice in the running of the enterprise. The vision was of a nation where theory and practice were united, and mental and physical work were shared, thereby dissolving the common class difference between workers and managers. The vision itself was a part of a grand narrative in which the "unconscious, irrational, conservative, past-orientated" tradition[10] would be replaced by "self-governing institutions composed of democratically elected, rotatable, recallable nonprofessional representatives of communes and producer collectives,"[11] where decisions would be made not by appeal to tradition but rather through rational dialogue that would serve the "long range interests of both

---

[7] Noam Chomsky and Robert Cohen, "Repression at Belgrade University," *New York Review of Books*, February 7, 1974.

[8] Walter Feinberg, "The Yugoslav Seven," *Christian Science Monitor*, March 17, 1981.

[9] The slogan was not unique to Yugoslavia.

[10] Mihailo Marković, "Equality and Social Autonomy," in W. Feinberg, ed., *Equality and Social Policy* (Urbana: University of Illinois Press, 1978), p. 93.

[11] Ibid., p. 95.

local communities and the whole federation."[12] In other words, praxis would guide political and economic practice by well-grounded rational theory. So what went wrong? Why did the center not hold?

The Background

Marković's reputation as a leading figure of Yugoslav socialism began during the Second World War when he was a partisan fighter under Tito, and it grew after the war when he and other young intellectual freedom fighters went into rural areas to promote their vision of a new socialist Yugoslavia. The goal, as Marković related it to me, was to help the population internalize this emerging national *Yugoslav* identity and to have its people see themselves first and foremost as Yugoslavs rather than, say, as Serbs or Croats. The idea was to grow a new country out of the many ethnic identities, stitching together the separate groups – Orthodox Serbs in Serbia, Roman Catholics in Croatia and Slovenia, Muslims and Orthodox in Bosnia and Herzegovina and Kosovo, and so on – into a unified, socialist country: Yugoslavia.

I was told that local, ethnic identities had developed out of very different and sometimes conflicting historical experiences. Serbia had been the western flank of the Ottoman Empire since the sixteenth century, while Croatia served as the eastern flank of the Hapsburg Empire. The two were frequently in conflict with one another. After the First World War, the two, along with members of other regions, nationalities, and religions, were amalgamated in an uneasy merger to form the country of Yugoslavia. The Second World War hardened these local identities further, pitting Serbs, who largely sided with the Allies, against Croatians, who were allied with Germany and the puppet regime it had established in the country. So even though Yugoslavia had formally been a country since 1922, the subjective consciousness and loyalties of its people remained divided. The political mission that occupied Marković and the Praxis group was to

---

[12] Ibid., p. 98.

change this – to create *one* Yugoslav identity out of the many local identities. Thus, after the war, even though Marković came to oppose many of Tito's policies, he remained a full-throated supporter of the Yugoslav nation, which he saw as an amalgamation of a number of different cultural and religious traditions, including Serbs and Croatians, Orthodox Christians and Muslims.

At the time of my 1974 visit, a united Yugoslavia seemed like the fulfillment of a utopian ideal, given the different stories that I heard from Serbs and Croats in informal settings, like bars and hotel restaurants. The memories were long. Serbs talked to me privately of the river having run red with the blood of Serbians during the Second World War, murdered by Croats allied with Germany. Croats complained about continuing Serbian domination. Yet to Marković and his Praxis colleagues, the unique Yugoslav practice of worker-managed enterprises gave their relatively new country something to be proud of, something that they hoped and believed would transcend old antagonisms and provide Yugoslavia with a new birth and a unique and democratic identity.

From the conclusion of the war to the time of my visit, Yugoslavia had made tremendous progress in education and economic development. For the first time in its history, compulsory, free schooling was available to everyone. Evening schools were available throughout the country, providing additional education and training for adults, often in their own ethnic language. And over 90 percent of the country was literate. Economically, Yugoslavia was being perceived as a regional leader. In the 1960s, its GDP grew at over 6 percent annually. Health care was free, and its market socialism was seen as a model by many who rejected both Soviet-style socialism and American capitalism.

The tragedy that became *the former* Yugoslavia started after Tito's death in 1980. Over a remarkably short period of time, the historical local identities – Serbs, Croats, Muslims, Orthodox Christians, and more – started to reassert themselves publicly, until the grand idea of one Yugoslav nation was overwhelmed by the collision of its different parts. There were many underlying causes for the split; high levels of unemployment and inflation were contributing factors, as was a decision by the Reagan administration to erect trade barriers that had the effect of reducing growth.[13] From the point of view of those committed to Yugoslavian socialism, it must have felt as if a giant tidal wave obliterated everything, leaving only high grounds – the former local allegiances – as islands in its wake. Marković and his Praxis colleagues were not spared. They, too, were swept up by their local ethnic identities, and along with it went their vision of one nation. The proposed story of one people was superseded by the many stories each told about a different and separate people without a unifying narrative. And stories about one promising future were superseded by stories of past conflicts and antagonism that went back hundreds of years.

Of course, as noted previously, the causes of the break-up were more complicated than simply a narrative lost. Rather, the lost narrative was both a result and a cause of other factors, such as economic downturn, external pressure, and uneven development. Serbia, less economically developed than Croatia and Slovenia, wanted more socialism; Croatia and Slovenia wanted more capitalism. Sectional conflicts that many people thought had been forgotten – such as Serbs versus Croats, Muslims versus Christians, and more – were rekindled in a kind of Hobbesian war of all against all. I recall my own shock some years after my visit, when I read in the *New York Times* that Marković was serving as a chief advisor to and apologist for the brutal Serbian president, Slobodan Milošević, who was later indicted for war crimes – he died of natural causes before his lawyers could finish their defense.

What had once seemed to be a miracle – the vision of a new kind of democratic socialism as an ideology that could unite the country –

---

[13] Milica Uvalic, "The Rise and Fall of Market Socialism in Yugoslavia," DOC Research Institute, March 27, 2018 (online); available at https://doc-research.org/2018/03/rise-fall-market-socialism-yugoslavia.

suddenly became a terrible nightmare. Both Croats and Serbs jealously saw the other as having enjoyed special privileges under Tito, privileges that they felt had been denied to them. Croatia, along with Slovenia, declared its separation and independence from Yugoslavia.

The shift was marked in the national consciousness by President Milošević's inflammatory 1989 St. Vitus Day speech. In that address, he reached back to the Slavs' defeat in Kosovo 600 years before, invoking the image of Serbian "victimhood." Tradition rose to bite reason, and the result was to intensify sectarian passions by provoking Serbian nationalism in the midst of the already smoldering conflict between Kosovo Serbs and Kosovo Albanians. And in the process, Marković the Yugoslav was replaced by Marković the Serb, joining with other Serbian intellectuals to advance the argument that Tito, himself a Croat, had designed postwar Yugoslavia to favor the Croats and exploit the Serbs by gerrymandering the shape of the different provinces. Marković became a prominent supporter of *Serbian* nationalism, a leading *Serbian* ideologue, and an active apologist of the Serbian leader Slobodan Milošević who would be indicted for crimes against humanity. What can we learn from the tragic history of Yugoslavia?

The Responsibility of the Office of Citizen

There is no doubt the *Yugoslav* Marković saw himself as a defender of both socialism and democracy. Worker-managed factories were meant to bring democratic practices down to the everyday working life of its citizens, and they were seen as a bolder democratic experiment than that of any of the Western democracies. The fact that Marković and his colleagues failed to stitch together competing local narratives into one national narrative shows just how difficult it can be, and how high a price may be paid by all concerned. They had placed their bet on a grand, speculative narrative that seemed to promise a better future but that did so while ignoring and dismissing as mere tradition the submerged cultural narratives of past conflict and repression.

The ultimate fate of Yugoslavia suggests that repressed narratives often do not go away, but they can remain as impediments to the most promising vision of the future. In attending to this future, Marković repressed the traditional stories of the different peoples who made up the Yugoslavia of his time. However, these stories were transmitted around dinner tables, in saloons, in barbershops, and in beauty parlors, where people met informally. Ultimately, the official stories authorized by the party, transmitted by the Praxis group during the Second World War and, after it was over, by formal educational institutions, were overwhelmed by the local stories about ethnic pride and external oppression and internal persecution.

The Humanities and the Grand Narrative

The Marković example allows us to see one of the reasons why suspicion of grand narratives might be called for. In the Yugoslav example, they served to dismiss as backward the local traditions that gave meaning to many people's lives. And, ironically, in the last analysis, Marković too – although he might not have admitted it – found meaning in his childhood identity as a Serb rather than in his later identity as a Yugoslav socialist. Yet his attraction to the grand narrative of history unfolding from warring traditions to a unified socialist democracy was not outlandish. However limited it may have been, it served as a source of hope. Some grand narratives do contain within themselves sources of great hope and progress, as well as the material for productive criticism.

The problem is not simply the grand narrative as such, but rather with the exclusionary functions they can serve – such as Marković's dismissal of tradition as irrational. And hence suspicion is the correct attitude, not about the fact of a grand narrative as such, but rather about its deployment for finality and its tendency to close off experience and dismiss meaningful lives that do not conform to the template it provides. What is needed, especially for countries like the United States where democracy is fractured but not yet completely broken, is an education that can open up settled narratives and take into account changing understanding of experience, both past and present, and for the sake of a more inclusive future. The object then is not to dismiss earlier forms of understanding as irrational but to locate the source of their limitations and the implicit assumptions that made them plausible for their time. Here the interpretive dimension of the humanities takes over from the speculative dimension. To illustrate, I reach back into my own early education experience and its limitations.

PART II   THE HUMANITIES AND STITCHING TOGETHER A NATIONAL NARRATIVE: THE USA

Mrs. Thompson and the Story of President Wilson

Mrs. [sic] Thompson was the most memorable teacher I had in public school. She never smiled until Christmas, but she was loved by March and remembered forever. She was my eighth-grade American history teacher at the Driscoll School in Brookline, Massachusetts, in the early 1950s. Each of her lessons was a performance. If we only knew that Washington crossed the Delaware to uproot the Hessian mercenaries at Trenton on Christmas Day, 1776 – knowledge that some today commercialize as "cultural capital" – she would have thought she failed us, as well as the entire Continental Army. Yes, we were expected to know those facts, as well as the reason for the crossing, but unless we also felt the soldiers' deep longing for their faraway families as they shivered on those open boats across that ice-packed river, she would say that we do not understand American history at all.

What sticks out most clearly in my mind are the lessons she taught about the life and contribution of President Woodrow Wilson. For Mrs. Thompson, Wilson was a tragic visionary, a near-great president, ranking just below Franklin Delano Roosevelt, defeated by his own body and by his myopic political enemies. According to her, the malicious but successful resistance of Senator Lodge and other Republican senators to Wilson's vision of one world acting with

American participation through a League of Nations "broke his heart" and contributed to his debilitating stroke. She also taught us that long after his death, Wilson's vision was eventually realized, through the formation of the United Nations with the United States as a charter member. As I mentioned before, Mrs. Thompson was never content with merely reciting names, events, and dates, although she did mention these; instead, she took pains to guide our empathy. She wanted us to get inside of Wilson's skin and to feel as he felt with each triumph and each defeat, and so she would act out his encounters with friend and foe. I came away with a deep appreciation of his contribution to both America and to the idea of a peaceful, interconnected world. She served well the role of an agent of collective national feeling – except for one detail that she neglected to tell us about Wilson: he was a racist.

My Shock

Many years later when I was teaching a course on the German philosopher, Jürgen Habermas and critical theory at the University of Illinois, I had reason to review Wilson's presidency and was shocked to find out that Wilson had premiered a racist film, *The Birth of a Nation* (1915), in the White House. For a while I still tried to reconcile this fact with the story of Wilson that I had learned from Mrs. Thompson. At first, I thought that Wilson must have been attracted to the cinematographic innovations of the film rather than to the glorification of the Klan or its depiction of Blacks as simpleminded and savage. As one recent critic commented:

> Problematically, "Birth of a Nation" wasn't just a seminal
> commercial spectacle but also a decisively original work of art – in
> effect, the founding work of cinematic realism, albeit a work that
> was developed to pass lies off as reality.[14]

---

[14] Richard Brody, "The Worst Thing about 'Birth of a Nation' Is How Good It Is," *New Yorker*, February 1, 2013 (online); available at www.newyorker.com/culture/richard-brody/the-worst-thing-about-birth-of-a-nation-is-how-good-it-is.

Given the story that I had learned in Mrs. Thompson's history class, I could only imagine the showing was an oversight by Wilson. And as bad as I believed that to be, I rejected the possibility that it represented conscious and deliberate racism, concluding it was an infatuation with the new technology.

In other words, I interpreted this new information through Mrs. Thompson's lens. Wilson was a good guy, almost a great one. Tragic certainly, but not bad, wicked, or evil. And thus he must have *intended* no harm by premiering the film. His sin must have been one of omission, not commission. However, in fact, as I learned later, he committed many other sins of commission, including resistance to women's suffrage, the suppression of war resisters, and the Red Scare.

Today, I think of Wilson differently. Wilson was likely a true racist, actively sharing many of the sentiments of D. W. Griffith, the director of *The Birth of a Nation*. The fact that Wilson premiered the film in the While House was not an oversight but consistent with his domestic policy. His government promoted white supremacy wherever it could, segregated the civil service and the armed forces, and named military bases after traitorous Southern Civil War generals and war criminals.[15] Today this understanding has overtaken Mrs. Thompson's benign picture of our twenty-eighth president, and Wilson's reputation is being downgraded. Even at his own institution, Princeton, Black students are forcing administrators to come to terms with his legacy by renaming buildings and programs that bear his name and by reinterpreting his contribution to that college and the country.[16] But at stake is more than just the name of a building or even the reputation of Wilson. The struggle over names of buildings at Princeton reflects the larger present struggle over a national identity, over the questions of who we are and just how we are to understand our past understanding of that past.

---

[15] *The New York Times*, July 12, 2020, p. 8.

[16] Eddie S. Glaude, Jr., *Begin Again: James Baldwin's America and Its Urgent Lessons for Our Own* (New York: Crown, electronic ed., 2020) p. 402 of 1033.

Today, what makes Mrs. Thompson memorable to me is not just that she presented a racist president as a hero, but rather that she was a good teacher, and it is because she was a good teacher that I do not want to besmirch my memory of her by defining her in terms of her treatment of Wilson. This tension in my own thought is not mine alone. It represents the tension in the nation as representatives of a racist past are being called out. If history is to be understood as more than simply one damn reinterpretation after another, and if the Marković problem of disunity is to be addressed, the tension needs to be reconciled and explained without eradicating our capacity for judgment.

The Interpretive Role of the Humanities

This then is the work of the interpretive dimension of the humanities. Its aim is to understand the intellectual horizon that gave rise to Mrs. Thompson's understanding of Wilson, without necessarily endorsing the worldview that Mrs. Thompson likely brought to her teaching. The task requires that we set aside our own judgment and the theories that inform them today in order to bring into focus the worldview that likely informed her presentation of Wilson in the early 1950's. This requires that brackets be temporarily placed around our own present understanding of race and racism if we are to see why she might have seen Wilson in such a favorable light, passing over the darker sides of his administration. Of course, once this is accomplished, then the brackets can be removed, and Wilson's actions can be used to test such ideas as structural racism and critical race theory. For now I want to give her the benefit of the doubt and to suggest that by ignoring Wilson's racism, she had no intention of endorsing it – although this was indeed her effect. Rather she had her eye on a different prize, and that drew her attention away from the racism in front of her.

How We Learn Not to See

But why did Mrs. Thompson not see this? Why did she ignore his racism? One simple answer is that the concept of racism itself is a relatively recent construction in the social science or educational literature and was not fully available to her generation. Look through the dictionaries of the twentieth century. The term does not appear until the 1930s and 1940s and is not commonly used until the 1960s when the Black Power Movement begins to make an impact on academic scholarship and popular culture.[17] Given this history, the right question is not, "Why did she ignore or paper it over?" This question presumes intentionality. Rather, the deeper question is, "Why could she not see it?" Or, if she did, "Why did she not treat it as problematic?"

One reasonable explanation is that as a schoolteacher, she occupied a relatively lowly position in the knowledge production industry. Above her was an impressive army of scholars, psychologists, and researchers who were making good careers trying to understand why "Negroes [sic] failed." These studies were supported by a prominent but deceptive paradigm[18] that ranked the intelligence of different groups of people and was used to justify restricting immigration from "less desirable" areas in Europe and Asia. Given the prominence of this paradigm, the contemporary concept of structural or institutional racism – racism due to dominant authorities and institutional practices and not innate individual differences – was not readily available to Mrs. Thompson. While she never condemned Wilson's racism, she never endorsed or tried to justify it either. Nor did she quite ignore it, since ignoring implies seeing and then turning away. Rather she simply did not see it. She was possibly aware of individual acts, segregating the armed forces and the civil service, naming of military bases after Southern generals and the like, the monuments being erected to the heroes of the South. Without a concept of structural racism, she did not have the intellectual tools needed to connect the dots, or to see that these events were related to the fact that not one

---

[17] See Feinberg, *What Is a Public Education*.

[18] Charles King, *Gods of the Upper Air: How a Circle of Renegade Anthropologists Reinvented Race, Sex, and Gender in the Twentieth Century* (New York: Doubleday, 2019).

Black student attended the Driscoll School – another example of not seeing. Had critical race theory been available to her, I would hope that her teaching would have been different – which may be one reason why this innovation has met with such resistance today.

Critical race theory advances a more complex view of racial inequality than the one available to Mrs. Thompson. Racial inequality is to be understood as the result of the intersection of subjective expectations and objective, historical conditions. This means that a person may hold no conscious animosity toward Black people and still be a racist. For example, in the early 1970s, my daughter had to be rushed to the emergency room, and I was surprised when a Black woman introduced herself as Dr. Graham and the young white male beside her as Matt, the nurse. My surprise was an indication that by taking the racial and gender hierarchies for granted, I had internalized a system of white privilege, even as I was working at the university to increase the number of African American students in the College of Education. But it was also the case that this experience – Black woman doctor/white male nurse – was an exception to the prevailing situation.

Structural racism, the nub of critical race theory, exists both in individuals and institutions as part of both the subjective and the objective environment. The concept of structural racism allows us to see this connection in new and productive ways, and it is a clear advance over other ways of viewing racial inequality, such as the result of an intellectual or cultural deficit.[19] It is a better theory, not just because, unlike the others, it avoids "blaming the victim," but because it enables new factors to be considered as contributing to racial differences in performance. Some of these are environmental factors, such as racial differences in the absorption of lead paint or polluted drinking water; some may be psychological, such as intergenerational trauma that can be traced back to the brutality of

[19] Walter Feinberg, *Understanding Education: Toward a Reconstruction of Educational Inquiry* (Cambridge: Cambridge University Press, 1983).

Jim Crow and slavery. Some are legal and economic, like the continuing impact of wealth accumulation from federal, state, and local housing discrimination; some are institutional, like racially biased police and partial immunity laws for police. Some are historical, such that during slavery it was illegal to teach slaves to read, and some are interactional, such that subjective expectations and objective institutional practices may serve to mutually reinforce one another.

Still, without an understanding of the dominant concerns of Mrs. Thompson's times – the Cold War and the hope placed in the newly founded United Nations – it would be difficult to grasp her admiration for Wilson. Wilson was her hero because he tried to create a world order that would address and possibly eliminate brutal wars, like the "Great War." He was tragic because he failed; without American participation, that structure – the League of Nations – was ineffective. Coming out of the Second World War, peace seemed like the greatest demand, while justice, in the form of the nascent Civil Rights Movement, was only beginning to take shape. The larger lesson to be drawn from this is that problems in the present shade how we view the past and what we take as important.

To understand all is not to forgive all. A fuller story would examine the way the myth of "the lost cause" was developed as one of the attempts to resubjugate formerly enslaved people by glorifying the Confederate cause (see Chapter 8). And a more complete story would consider the acts of those who continued to attempt to subordinate "Negroes," often for their own narrow benefit! There are real evils to be found. With twenty-twenty hindsight and at some later date, progressives might well find fault with our own favored explanations, such as structural racism or critical race theory, where the words of W. E. B. Du Bois, written during the earlier part of the last century, might seem morally appropriate:

Our histories tend to discuss American slavery so impartially, that in the end nobody seems to have done wrong and everyone was right. Slavery appears to have been thrust upon unwilling helpless America, while the South was blameless in becoming its center ... One is astonished in the study of history at the recurrence of the idea that evil must be forgotten, distorted, skimmed over.[20]

For Du Bois the moral dimension of slavery must remain front and center:

> The most terrible thing about war, I am convinced, is its monuments – the awful things we are compelled to build in order to remember its victims. In the South, particularly, human ingenuity has been put to it to explain on its war monuments, the Confederacy. Of course, the plain truth of the matter would be an inscription something like this: "Sacred to the memory of those who fought to Perpetuate Human Slavery." But that reads with increasing difficulty as time goes on. It does, however, seem to be overdoing the matter to read on a North Carolina Confederate monument: "Died Fighting for Liberty."[21]

A Future for the Humanities

Jill Lepore, in her short but compelling case for American nationhood, *This Is America: The Case for the Nation*, defines America as "a community of belonging, held together by the strength of our ideals and by the force of our disagreements."[22] She holds, as do I, that a new Americanism would rest on a history that "tells the truth, as best it can, about what W. E. B. Du Bois called the hideous mistakes, the frightful wrongs, and the great and beautiful things that nations do."[23] Lepore quotes Frederick Douglass, the former slave, to state the case for a nation committed to the advancement of human rights; he saw a

---

[20] As quoted in Clint Smith, *How the Word Is Passed: A Reckoning with the History of Slavery across America* (New York: Little, Brown, 2021), p. 101.

[21] W. E. B. Du Bois, as quoted in ibid., p. 145.

[22] Jill Lepore, *This Is America: The Case for the Nation* (New York: Liveright, 2019), p. 136.

[23] Ibid., p. 137.

nation of different peoples, what he called "composite nationalities" to be "not the nation's weakness but its strength."[24] Remarkably Douglass made these remarks only a few years after the end of the Civil War when the Black population was trying to gain its footing as enslaved no longer and when other groups were feeling the brunt of oppression. Lepore continues to quote Douglass: "I want a home here not only for the negro, the mulatto and the Latin races; but I want the Asiatic to find a home here in the United States, and feel at home here, both for his sake and for ours."[25]

Lepore writes as a historian, and the task of the historian is to *tell* the truth. But telling the truth is not the whole story. There is the need to *receive* the truth in a way that is consistent with democracy. The task of the educator, while complementary, is quite different from that of the historian. The educator's role is to *prepare* a people to hear and respond to truth that may not always be easy to hear. The humanities as an interpretive study is critical for developing the skills required to both hear and respond to uncomfortable truths by probing the interpretive frames that can help understand the source of such discomfort. From the standpoint of a "composite national" identity, the humanities defined as the source of interpretive understanding and critical engagement are the most important subject areas for a democratic education because they can set the stage for collective discussions about who we are and who we might like to become. In other words, the humanities provide the material for collective self-understanding and development.

[24] Ibid., p. 67.   [25] Ibid., p. 68.

5 The Humanities

Interpretation, Judgment, and the Evolution of National Narratives

> I love America more than any other country in the world and, exactly for this reason, I insist on the right to criticize her perpetually.

James Baldwin, *Notes of a Native Son* (Boston: Beacon Press, 1955)

NATIONAL NARRATIVES AND DEMOCRACY

National narratives are constructed and revised with an aim toward maintaining national cohesion by promoting an image of continuity of past, present, and future. Images of America as a "City on a Hill," of the American Dream, or the land of continuous progress have provided material for sustaining this continuity across generations, often despite experiences that counter the official story. Today the conflict over the character of the national narrative is visible in the resistance to the teaching inspired by critical race theory and other forms of anti-racism in schools. Not too long ago, *The New York Times* reported on the resistance to teaching about systemic racism, sometimes labeled "critical race theory."

> In Loudoun County, Va., a group of parents led by a former Trump appointee are pushing to recall school board members after the school district called for mandatory teacher training in "systemic oppression and implicit bias."
>
> In Washington, 39 Republican senators called history education that focuses on systemic racism a form of "activist indoctrination."
>
> And across the country, Republican-led legislatures have passed bills recently to ban or limit schools from teaching that racism is infused in American institutions.[1]

---

[1] Trip Gabriel and Dana Goldstein, "Disrupting Racism's Reach, Republicans Rattle American Schools," *The New York Times*, June 1, 2021.

In the name of patriotism, reactionary legislators from Texas to New Hampshire are promoting an exclusionary form of patriotism, one that seeks social cohesion by intimidating and silencing alternative voices and lifestyles. Here the patriot is but a cheerleader glorifying the nation's past.

In contrast to the cheerleading patriot, the new patriots are neither warrior nor cheerleader. They are custodians who take on the everyday responsibility of caring for democratic institutions and relationships. Caring involves attending to the adequacy of the national narrative – the story a people tell themselves about themselves. Of course there is more than one unified narrative, and different stories compete with one another for time and space in the curriculum and elsewhere. And this means taking care to craft and safeguard the more adequate narratives, while shedding additional light on the sources and continuing appeal of less adequate ones. But then the questions arise, just what is "the more adequate interpretation," and how can we determine that one interpretation is to be preferred over another? Let's return to Mrs. Thompson's treatment of Wilson to begin to answer this question in a way that both acknowledges its deficits and provides her with the benefit of the doubt by looking beyond her personal intentions and to the conceptual tools available to her at the time.

I want to suggest that compared to narratives that enable a diagnostic analysis of American history, which critical race theory has the potential to do, the narrative she drew upon was deficient because the concept of racism itself, a concept crucial to a more critical understanding of the Black experience in America and to understanding America itself, was in the very early stages of its development at the time she taught. (Elsewhere I have documented how the concept developed slowly, not appearing as entries in official sources like dictionaries and encyclopedia until the middle of the twentieth century.[2]) This absence meant that while there were a lot

---

[2] Feinberg, *What Is a Public Education.*

of dots presented (slavery, Jim Crow, poll taxes, etc.), they were not fully connected. The concept of racism developed out of the many dots and, at the same time, allowed the dots to be corrected and projected on to the present and the future (e.g., housing and educational discrimination in the North as well as in the South), and critical race theory draws on these connections today.

So as middle school students, we did learn about slavery, Jim Crow, poll taxes, and other features of continuing oppression; however, we did not learn of them in terms of oppression, nor did we learn about their continuing effects. Instead, flawed theories of racial, intellectual, or cultural differences were used to support alternative explanations, which in turn were promulgated through the contemporary biology texts.[3] Hence, a prevailing view was that since slavery was over, the condition of "the Negro" was their own doing. The advantage of including the element of conceptual deficit into an analysis of the national narratives on race is that it allows us to better understand just what is systematic about *systematic* racism, and by doing so, we are better able to place competing theories in conversation with one another. And, of course, it encourages exploration of the extension of racism beyond the boundaries of the South to the many complicit acts of the North. But this advance requires that we change our understanding of meaning from a fundamentalist to a dialogical view.

A DIALOGICAL VIEW OF MEANING

A dialogical view suggests that the meaning of an idea or event emerges by placing competing narratives in conversation with one another. Whether one narrative is more adequate than another will depend on a number of factors, such as whether it can account for and explain both the insights and anomalies of a competitor (e.g., all men are created equal – except Blacks and women) and whether it can account for new and unexpected experiences, such as Thomas

---

[3] Feinberg, *Understanding Education.*

Jefferson's encounter with the brilliant Black mathematician Benjamin Banneker.[4]

To see this, return to the example of Wilson and ask two questions: First, what is it that makes the understanding of Wilson as a racist more adequate than Mrs. Thompson's view that he was a tragic hero and near-great president? Second, what are the implications for the education of the custodians of democracy of the view that *progress* in interpretation is possible and that we can reasonably determine that some interpretations are more adequate than others. Eddie Glaude Jr. spells out the stakes of failing to acknowledge and identify inadequate interpretations:

> One of the unique features of American nationalism is how closely interwoven the idea of America is with the individual identity of white people in this county. American history corroborates a particular sense of the self rooted in liberty, self-reliance, and hard work. That history validates who white Americans take themselves to be, and the lives they lead, in turn, validate the specialness of America itself and its mission to the world.... To say then that the idea of white America is irredeemable is the equivalent of removing the stone that keeps our sense of ourselves in place. Without the idea, the whole house comes tumbling down. But if we don't rid ourselves of the idea of white America, we seal our fate.
>
> If the condition of the love of country is a lie, the love itself, no matter how genuine, is a lie. It disfigures who we are because we engage in self-deceit. In the end, we have to free ourselves of the hold and allure of such a self-deceiving love because that is the only way we can imagine ourselves anew and love truly.[5]

Mrs. Thompson's Wilson fits the traditional story that Americans – at least some white people – told themselves about the "City on a Hill"

---

[4] See Michael Meyerson, *Political Numeracy: Mathematical Perspectives on Our Chaotic Constitution* (New York: W. W. Norton, 2002), pp. 130–131.

[5] Eddie S. Glaude Jr., *Begin Again: James Baldwin's America and Its Urgent Message for Our Own* (New York: Crown, electronic ed., 2020), p. 417 of 1033.

that served as an example for all who longed for a new beginning. For her, Wilson's goodness was embodied in his innocence and his vulnerability to the assault of nativist Republicans. He offered the Old World a new beginning, but one that was ultimately rejected by cynical forces at home and self-serving actors abroad.

Note I say "some white people," as opposed to Glaude's "white people," because I fear that his label can serve to obscure the real-life situation of many immigrant groups who arrived in the country not as white, but as Irish, Italian, Greek, and so on, who only generations later grew into whiteness. Moreover, the idea that white people as a whole held a certain view is stereotypic and conceals important complexities. Nevertheless, Glaude's larger point still stands: The ability to enter into whiteness bestowed many privileges denied to Black people.

Glaude does not say just how we are to identify or eliminate an inadequate national story, nor does he say *how* to respond to those who resist and hold on to a distorted interpretation of the past. Here the humanities can play an important part by providing rising citizens with a critical understanding of competing narratives and with the conceptual tools they will need to take account of emerging future clashes.

SHOCK AS A TEACHING MOMENT

Shock, the sudden upheaval of normal expectations and experience, such as the experience I felt when I learned that Wilson premiered *The Birth of a Nation* in the White House, can be a powerful teacher. It can disrupt dysfunctional habits and challenge inflexible ideas leading to individual and collective growth. However, if handled poorly, it leads to retrenchment and the embrace of old familiar patterns of behavior and comfortable ideas.

Shock arises from sources that disrupt the existing system of thoughts, habits, traditions, and customs, systems that allow life to be lived relatively smoothly. By straining well-developed patterns of thought and behavior, the initial response to shock is one of confusion in thought and paralysis in action. Sudden cultural change is one of the most common reasons for shock. As people's neighbors change, especially when the change is rapid, they may feel their language is being distorted and their way of life is being discounted. The grocer no longer speaks Yiddish, but the new one now speaks Spanish. The old kosher deli has disappeared, replaced by a ribs joint. The sounds and smells are all different, the familiar neighbors have all moved out, and the synagogue has been sold to a Catholic mission. The jokes are not the same. The historical memories are different. The cultural references are met with blank stares. Old habits no longer work, or they work but in an ever-decreasing communal range.

You are literally becoming dysfunctional because your cultural and linguistic tools of functioning are leaving you. You have been left behind, and unless you change, permanent alienation is the likely consequence. But given the extended range of media, cultural change is no longer just a neighborhood affair. It can have national implications. Nevertheless, alienation can be a natural part of the process of cultural reflection, allowing people to begin the process of extending empathy beyond their cultural boundaries.

CULTURAL SELF-PITY AND PROJECTION

Cultural self-pity is a collective mindset that freezes cultural development at a certain point in time, self-defined as suffering and oppression, and limits empathy to members of one's own group. We saw an example of cultural self-pity in Chapter 4 with Yugoslav president Milošević's inflammatory 1989 St. Vitus Day speech referring to an event that took place more than 600 years ago. But misplaced cultural self-pity plays an important role in the recent history of the United States as well. Consider the following remark by the late Justice Scalia in providing a justification for his rejection of affirmative action:

> My father came to this country when he was a teenager. Not only had he never profited from the sweat of any Black man's brow, I don't think he had ever seen a Black man. There are, of course,

many white ethnic groups that came to this country in great numbers relatively late in its history – Italians, Jews, Poles – who not only took no part in, and derived no profit from, the major historical suppression of the currently acknowledged minority groups, but were, in fact, themselves the objects of discrimination by the dominant Anglo-Saxon majority. To be sure, in relatively recent years some or all of these groups have been the beneficiaries of discrimination against Blacks, or have themselves practiced discrimination, but to compare their racial debt ... with that of those who plied the slave trade, and who maintained a formal caste system for many years thereafter, is to confuse a mountain with a molehill.[6]

As a justice of the US Supreme Court, Scalia was a staunch opponent of affirmative action, and while he justified his opposition by questionable appeals to the Constitution, cultural self-pity played an oversize role in his opinions. We don't need to reject the fact of anti-Italian discrimination and worse – in fact, one of the largest single acts of lynching, if defined narrowly as hanging, in this county occurred when eleven Italian men were murdered by a mob in New Orleans in 1891 – in order to challenge the logic behind Scalia's narrative and the claim that he never profited from Black labor, either before or after the Civil War.

COUNTERFACTUAL THINKING AND RETHINKING THE NATIONAL NARRATIVE

It is possible that Scalia's father "never saw a Black man," but it is more likely that Scalia's father never really *saw* a Black man because he never chose to *look*. Much more improbable is the claim that he "never profited from the sweat of any Black man's brow," especially given the discrimination in government-backed mortgage programs and other private and public policies that favored white people over

---

[6] "In His Own Words," *The New York Times*, June 19, 1986, D, p. 27.

Black people, allowing whites to build up capital and wealth. But here Scalia is simply making a historical error that could be corrected by presenting the evidence on the role of racial discrimination on capital accumulation. Counterfactual thinking reveals a different and deeper level of truth. It is sometimes claimed that without slave labor, the South could not have developed, and as a result, the growth of the country would have been stunted. Accepting this claim for the sake of argument, let's imagine a fair system of deciding who would be slave and who free. The fairest method would likely have been a kind of arbitrary selection, where enslaved people would be selected randomly without regard to race.[7]

In 1860, on the eve of the Civil War, an estimated 13 percent of the total population was enslaved, about 43 percent of the population in the hot, underdeveloped, disease-ridden Deep South. Suppose, instead of enslaving people because of their skin color, all people who ever wished to emigrate to America (Irish, Italian, Poles, etc.) would have their names drawn at random, and about 13 percent would be chosen to be enslaved, while the rest would be allowed to live freely. Would Scalia's father have chosen to risk his well-being and the well-being of his children in the slave lottery? If not, then Scalia failed to understand that he and his father owed a great deal to the Black man his father "had never seen."

Yet we can see that a great deal is at stake for Scalia personally in the story he internalized. At stake were both Scalia's view that he and his family had made it on their own and his view of America as a country where anyone, given the intelligence and desire, could make it too. The implicit conclusion was that affirmative action was an undeserved handout, which at best would serve to dampen motivation.

Scalia's story resonates with many people and part of the reason is that much of it reflects the real experience of European immigrants.

---

[7] This thought experiment is inspired by John Rawls, *A Theory of Justice* (Cambridge: Harvard University Press, 1974).

They worked hard, were often exploited, and, over generations, many were able to rise out of poverty. However, the story, while not false, is not the whole truth either, especially when it is used to divert attention from the continuing discrimination exercised against Black people. Dialogical interpretation can allow for a generous interpretation of such narratives without surrendering truth to the purpose of misguided collective self-pity. Generosity calls for rising citizens to interpret past understandings, as they would want their own narrations, warts and all, to be interpreted in the future. A shared national story needs to weave together conflicting narratives into a coherent story, sometimes by challenging the logic that supports self-pity narratives, but without ignoring the experience that they serve to memorialize, or ignoring significant differences that may call for distinct kinds of recognition.

THE HUMANITIES AND THE CREATION OF SHARED STORIES

The rising citizen then has two tasks that require the broader understanding provided by the humanities. The first is to learn how to identify stories that serve to promote misguided collective self-pity by deconstructing them, opening them up, and examining the images they convey, the feelings they provoke, the audience for which they were created, and the alternative possibilities they may conceal. As part of this, the humanities should also serve to reveal how and why stories originated and the truths they contain. The second task is to build new layers of interpretation that incorporate new knowledge and changing conditions. The task of interpretation then for the custodians is "to use history ... to think about and guide the future."[8] Everything else being equal, the best interpretation of the past for advancing democracy in the present is one that serves to light the way for a more inclusive, more democratic future.

---

[8] Neil MacGregor, as quoted by Susan Neiman, *Learning from the Germans: Race and the Memory of Evil* (New York: Farrar, Straus and Giroux, electronic ed., 2019), Chapter 1.

HUMANITIES: REFLECTION AND THE ROLE OF CONTEXT

The humanities are concerned with opening up meanings that have been frozen and to encourage alternative interpretations. Interpretations differ, but the more adequate interpretation will be able to explain the particular problems that the alternative is unable to adequately address and the source of its limitation. For example, sometimes the meaning of a picture will be ambiguous until the interest of the interpreter is clarified. The philosopher Ludwig Wittgenstein makes this point in his famous example of the duck/ rabbit image that he presented in his *Philosophical Investigations*.[9] The figure could be seen as either a duck or a rabbit, and the perception will often change back from one to the other. However, given different interests, the image is likely to stabilize in a certain way. If the viewer were a gardener with rabbit problems or if the picture were placed in a flower garden, it is more likely it would be seen as a rabbit, but if it were placed in a pond and shown to a duck hunter, it would likely be seen as a duck. In other words, context, including the context that encompasses the experience of the viewer, will likely shape the way the ambiguity – duck or rabbit – is resolved. More to the point, to understand clashing interpretations may involve understanding the different ongoing activities of the viewer because, over time, context can change and so can meaning.

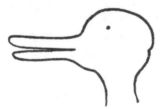

The recognition of ambiguity is a call for reflection and of opening up different possibilities in order to gain perspective.

---

[9] Ludwig Wittgenstein, *Philosophical Investigations*, 3rd ed. (New York: Macmillan Co., 1958), p. 194.

Gaining perspective is the process of bringing context, normally a background factor, into focus. Once meaning is fixed for a given purpose, the context may again recede to the background. Perspective has both a spatial dimension (here and there) and a temporal dimension (now and then). Meaning is dependent on both. The artist steps back from her painting to better see how lines, color, and brush stroke cohere at a certain distance, that of a future viewer. Given distance in time, the historian will see things that the journalist did not – including the stories then told by journalists and the historical context that influenced the journalist. When we reflect on a text, even if in private, we seek to understand it from various viewpoints, trying to bring different perspectives together and to understand the changes that occurred. "I used to see the lines as a duck but then I saw the field – obviously a rabbit."

Progress in interpretation involves understanding the factors that give rise to new insights and taking them into account in evaluating older or discarded perceptions. The mistake relativists make is their failure to comprehend that the aim of inquiry is not to provide an exact replica of the thing – neither duck, nor rabbit – but to provide a better interpretation of events, and this involves a clearer sense of the background factors that bring one or another explanation to prominence. A better viewpoint is one that can give an adequate account of competing concepts, and the reasons for them. Progress in interpretation also entails understanding purpose. The gardener and the hunter each look through the lens of their own history, so an even more complete interpretation occurs when they each understand how their own biography – as gardener or hunter – influences the ideas they advance. Conflicting interpretations can exist side by side, while at the same time providing an invitation to examine more closely the differences in context and purpose that comprise the background conditions of those differences. And for the custodian of democracy, it calls for an articulation of the implications that the different points of view have for key democratic values, such as inclusiveness, equality, liberty, community, and happiness. And these may differ given the demands of different historical periods.

THE HUMANITIES ACROSS GENERATIONS

The goal of the humanities, from the standpoint of the office of the custodian of democracy, is to assemble a democratic, inclusive narrative out of local narratives, one that advances the basic ideals of democracy, freedom, equality, community, and happiness. Given the clash of possible interpretations, some better than others, some quite equal in merit, how do we avoid the Marković problem where the national narrative dissolves when replaced by local, conflicting stories? Or to return to the James Baldwin quote with which I began this chapter, is it really an option to both love deeply and criticize perpetually? Or, why should he continue to love America after it has so consistently disappointed him?

I want to suggest that the love that Baldwin expresses is more than just a love of one for another, like the love of one married partner for another. It is a love not just of the individual but of the relationship as well. In other words, it is the kind of love through which each is constituted and through which each is changed. When they love each other through their marriage, they want each other to grow, both independently and together, through their relationship, and they want their relationship itself to develop and mature. I want to suggest that the best way to understand Baldwin's love of country is by analogy to the couple who, by loving their marriage, continue to reconstitute it – even when they disagree. This means that a critical love for country is an awesome responsibility and calls for a new breed of patriot. Without criticism, it ceases to grow. Without love, it ceases to be. Take them away and you have the Marković problem.

6   STEM and the Democratic Aims of Mathematics Education

INTRODUCTION

Mathematics education presents two challenges for the custodians of democracy. The first is to promote equal opportunity; mathematics is a major factor in the selection of candidates for advanced education and for many rewarding professions. The task for custodians is to promote fair selection procedures, ones where present performance is relevant to future responsibilities and where irrelevant factors, like parental income or background, or excessive and unnecessary requirements, do not intrude on selection. The second challenge is to nurture specific qualities of democratic culture and thought, qualities that can promote both inquiry and openness. These two challenges are related, but the first is the more familiar one, and so I will begin with that.

THE FIRST CHALLENGE: SELECTION AND OPPORTUNITY

Math has a reputation for separating the weak lambs from the powerful lions – hardly a democratic image. In many math classrooms, the same few students always have their hands up, ready with the correct answer to the toughest problem, while the others hide – heads down, staring at their desks – hoping not to be called on as they belatedly struggle to understand the solution to the last problem. In the teacher's lounge, there is the buzz about the math whiz and whether he – and it was usually a *he* – will choose MIT or Cal Tech, Stanford or one of the Ivies. And there is the sad collective shrug expressing pity for the student who is fated to "never really get it." Students are marked by the kind of math they take – smart kids take advanced trig and calculus, and the slow ones take general or consumer math. And these markers have wider consequences in terms of the attention students receive, the clubs they belong to, their friends, and their future vocational choices.

> One of the issues of math in the curriculum is the role that algebra and calculus play. Both are gatekeeper or choke points in the curriculum. Algebra is the first big one, separating the sheep from the goats in middle school. Many kids don't pass it or go no further. Then calculus in high school separates those deemed capable of science from those who aren't. You might be amazed at how much filtering these do. Algebra feels hard because it is more abstract, being based on variables, like x, y and z, rather than specific numbers. Calculus is confusing because it introduces very new symbols, like those for differentiation or integration.[1]

Subjects in the school curriculum project a certain amount of status, both high and low, and advanced math is at the top. Students internalize that status in terms of their own self-image and sense of future possibilities.

> Many math professors are protective of this status. They understandably do not want to see their subject watered down or distorted for the sake of a positive self-image. "You can get your positive image in other ways." Others, especially some progressive math education professors, are understandably protective of the student and fear a poor performance in math can contribute to the development of a negative self-image. For many, on both sides, the problem is social, as well as individual, and contributes to racial disparity and inequality.

> There are, for example, persistent race gaps on the math section of the SAT, which is an important gateway to higher education. Insofar as SAT scores predict student success in college, inequalities in SAT score distributions reflect and reinforce racial inequalities across generations.

[1] Correspondence from Eric Bredo, December 11, 2021.

Analyzing data published by the College Board for college-bound seniors in 2015, we find very large racial achievement gaps. Blacks and Latinos remain clustered at the very bottom of the distribution. Blacks in particular lag far behind, with an average score of 428 out of 800, significantly below the average score of 534 for whites and 598 for Asians.[2]

The gatekeeping role of math reaches back into the early grades and forward into graduate schools and professional colleges. For the most part, a student needs high grades in advanced math courses to get accepted into many of the better universities in the country, and then into high prestige professional colleges, and this may well be the case even when the student's major and future profession will have little to do with proficiency in math.

EQUALITY OF OPPORTUNITY

Equality of opportunity is generally accepted as a fundamental aim of democratic education. The ideal of equality of opportunity is simple: For every *relevant* merit point on a given skill or intelligence scale, there is a corresponding reward point on a parallel occupational task and pay scale. Relevance is determined by the functional connection between the skill as measured and the occupational task that it screens for. Reasonable equal opportunity is one of the conditions for a well-functioning democracy. Any systematic mismatch between potential merit and future reward is a sign of imperfection that needs correcting.

However, this simple formula leaves many openings for distortion. One of the signs of a dysfunctional democracy is the use of artificial proxies that favor children of already privileged parents. One famous non-Western historical example is the very rigorous test that was required for positions in the Chinese literati that served

---

[2] Richard V. Reeves, "Race Gap in SAT Math Scores Are as Big as Ever," February 1, 2017 (online); available at www.brookings.edu/blog/brown-center-chalkboard/2017/02/01/race-gaps-in-sat-math-scores-are-as-big-as-ever.

classical China for 2,000 years prior to the upheavals of the twentieth century. Theoretically, the tests were open to all, but they were so exacting and required so much preparation time that only the children of elite parents had the leisure required to study for them.[3] Nevertheless, the apparent openness and objectivity of the test served to legitimize the Chinese bureaucracy for many people, while also assuring the reproduction of a rigid class system with very limited intergenerational mobility.

The literati example raises a number of similar concerns for modern democracies and especially for the way mathematics is used as a screening device. For example, given the appropriateness of mathematics for selection to high-quality university programs and professional schools, the unequal quality of math education in grade school and high school is a serious concern for democracy. There is often a big difference between the math available in wealthy suburban schools and the math available in inner city and minority schools. Much of this difference is hidden in plain sight, hence enabling social-class reproduction while presenting an illusion of fairness.

In addition to the disparity in math education between wealthy and poor school districts, there is the question of whether the math requirement is really an appropriate proxy for future performance or whether it simply serves to exclude otherwise appropriate candidates from entering prized occupational fields. For example, some critics hold that the calculus requirement for medical school or business school is unnecessary and serves to arbitrarily eliminate otherwise qualified candidates from competing for spaces. Similarly, the requirement for algebra for entrance into colleges has its critics. As Hersh and John-Steiner note, "[O]nce out of school, hardly anybody has to solve a quadratic equation or prove a geometry theorem."[4] They ask, "Do you

---

[3] Max Weber, *From Max Weber: Essays in Sociology* (London: Routledge, 2009), chapter xvii.

[4] Reuben Hersh and Vera John-Steiner, *Loving and Hating Mathematics: Challenging the Myths of Mathematical Life* (Princeton: Princeton University Press, 2011), p. 319.

know of a doctor, lawyer, or businessperson who uses calculus, or even an algebraic equation or a theorem from geometry?"[5]

From the point of view of democracy, there are all kinds of good reasons for teaching math, but if Hersh and John-Steiner are right that math serves as an artificial barrier for entrance into a valued university or occupation, then it is being used for undemocratic ends. However, Hersh and John-Steiner are not denying the value of math. Rather they are questioning its application for signaling merit in many areas. They conclude:

> It is unrealistic and unnecessary to guarantee that every child pass 10th grade algebra, and have good facility with quadratic equations or with systems of two and three linear equations. What is necessary is that every child have the opportunity to learn algebra, in a well-equipped classroom from a qualified, highly motivated teacher.[6]

They add, "At the university level, we believe that no one can be considered educated who does not have some appreciation of mathematical thinking and its importance to science."[7] Appreciation, however, should not be confused with application.

THERE IS MORE TO DEMOCRACY THAN EQUAL OPPORTUNITY

Equality of opportunity, even when functioning smoothly, is not all there is to democracy. The match between a present performance and future reward does not address critical questions, such as how much difference between reward points is fair or how those rewards should be decided. In other words, while equal opportunity is a necessary condition for a democratic ideal, it is not sufficient. As Chapters 1–5 have shown, democracy requires certain habits of thought and culture, and in the next section, I explore the contribution math can

[5] Ibid.   [6] Ibid., p. 322.   [7] Ibid., p. 323.

make to developing these habits, as well as some of the roadblocks math education may place in front of them.

MATH AND HABITS OF THOUGHT AND CULTURE

Consider the following example presented to teachers; I invite you to participate:

> First, divide the fraction 1 3/4 by 1/2.
> Second, describe how you arrived at the answer.

Here are some responses from elementary school teachers when asked to complete the same problem:

1. "The first thing you'd have to do is change them into sync. Well, you're supposed to multiply that and add that. So that's 4, plus it's 7/4, and then you have to make it the same. Divide by 2/4 Right? And then you just cross multiply like that. You get 28/8."
2. "For some reason it is in the back of my mind that you invert one of the fractions. Like you know 7/4 becomes 4/7, or ½ becomes 2/1. I am not sure."
3. "I would try to find, oh goodness, the lowest common denominator, I would change them both. Lowest common denominator, I think that is what it is called. I don't know how I am going to get the answer. Whoops. Sorry."[8]

REFLECTION AND THE FORMATION
OF A DEMOCRATIC MINDSET

Clearly the teachers are stumped, which may not be all that unusual, but notice that their response reveals a rigid conception of what mathematics is: "You're *supposed* to," as if the rule were enforcing itself; or "For some reason" as in I don't really know why I am *supposed* to do what I am *supposed* to do; or the simple "Whoops. Sorry." A remark you might make after accidentally stepping on a person's toes. Here the rule serves as a strict enforcer whose violation

---

[8] From Liping Ma, *Knowing and Teaching Elementary Mathematics: Teachers' Understanding of Fundamental Mathematics in China and the United States* (Mahwah: Lawrence Erlbaum, 1999), pp. 56–58.

has personal consequences. None of the teachers think to stop to figure out precisely what they are being asked to do. This is not that surprising given the way math is often taught as a set of invariable algorithmic steps to be followed unquestionably.

When I recall my own struggle learning to divide fractions, I can understand the likely source of the teachers' response, and I also can see some of the lost opportunities to use math to develop habits of democratic thinking. The following is a loose rendition of my sixth-grade lesson in dividing fractions that occurred over seventy years ago:

> Mrs. Perry, setting the problem up on the board: What is 1/2 divided by 1/4?
> Mrs. Perry, explaining the steps we needed to follow to solve it:

First, let the first fraction 1/2 stand as it is and then

1. Change the division sign to a multiplication sign.
2. Take the second fraction and invert it so that the 4 is on the top and the 1 on the bottom.
3. Multiply the top numbers of the two fractions together. These are called the numerators.
4. Multiply the bottom numbers of the two fractions together. These are called the denominators.

Mrs. Perry: Does anyone want to try it?

Sam, the best math student in the class, is the first to raise his hand. He steps up to the board, writing:

$$\tfrac{1}{2} \div \tfrac{1}{4}.$$

$$\tfrac{1}{2} \times \tfrac{4}{1} = \tfrac{4}{2}.$$

Mrs. Perry: can you simplify that any further?

Sam writes:

$$4 \div 2 = 2.$$

Mrs. Perry: Very nice. She then hands a piece of yellow paper to each student and tells us to solve for a different problem that she writes on the board.

I recall sitting for a long time and staring confusedly at that blank sheet of paper, while thinking: It says divide, so why is she telling us to multiply? I thought that ¼ was one-fourth of a whole, now I am told it is four wholes.

This made no sense to me. Mrs. Perry comes around and looks at my blank paper, I sense (or imagine?) a quiet sigh of disappointment, and she moves on.

So Sam succeeds because he ignores everything we have been taught about division up to this point (i.e., when you see a ÷ sign, divide!), while I am paralyzed because my initial intuitions, developed out of past lessons on division, is in direct conflict with the orders I am now being given. Could this be some kind of trick? Probably not, since Sam is praised while he discards past instructions in favor of the most recent set of orders.

Still I feel I am the object of subtle disapproval because I cannot resolve the contradiction: To divide or to multiply? That is the question! Should I do what I think is right, or do I follow Mrs. Perry's orders? I am stuck no matter which option I choose. My paralysis is the result of being presented with a Hobbesian choice: violate my own best understanding or violate an order issued from on high. (Could it be that the apology by subject 3 earlier was the result of the same kind of bewilderment?) In the end, I follow Sam's lead and learn to sublimate my intuitions and accept the fact that rules of math are indifferent to what I think they should be. So I never even thought to ask:

1. Why is it legitimate to turn a division sign into a multiplication sign?
2. How can ¼ suddenly become 4/1s or 4?
3. What is being multiplied when numerators are multiplied together and then denominators?
4. Why is the quotient larger than the dividend?

Granted, for many purposes, teaching students to apply a simple algorithm is sufficient. (The rules of math are largely indifferent to what I think of them.) For other purposes perhaps not so much.

However, the right answer serves a different purpose when the aim is to prepare students to serve as custodians of democracy than it does when the aim is, say, to produce informed consumers or more efficient bakers. In the former, transparency is a critical part of the aim. We want citizens to be aware of the connection between learning how to follow rules and the reason the rule works the way it does. With this aim in mind, the *right* answer functions not as *the aim* of the exercise but as a constraint that helps the student examine their own thought processes in a collaborative way, both with the teacher and with other students. "Ideally math it's not just about applying algorithms but about understanding why and how."[9] The advantage of going beyond the algorithm is much like the advantage of fixing a car when you know how the engine works but the usual routine steps to fix it prove to be inadequate. Such knowledge enables a flexible response to unfamiliar problems.

FLEXIBILITY, RULES, AND THE VALUE OF MISTAKES

Conceptual flexibility refers to the capacity to follow the reasoning that leads to a stated conclusion, as well as the capacity to consider problems from a different point of view. Flexibility is critical for the workings of democracy because responsible citizenship requires the capacity to listen to reason and, when appropriate, to change one's mind. Developing the kind of flexibility appropriate to democracy involves a certain kind of relationship to rules, one where we normally give the existing rule the benefit of the doubt, but where we also reserve the right to judge the rule's applicability to a given circumstance. The label "officious" is reserved for people who are so rule-bound they cannot consider any possible exceptions. A democratic mindset understands the importance of rules but is ready to question them when they don't seem to make sense, either in themselves or for the situation at hand. A democratic math

---

[9] Eric Bredo comment on draft of chapter.

education needs to promote conceptual flexibility by helping students determine the fitness of a given approach to the circumstances.

FLEXIBILITY IN MATH

Rather than rigidly following rules, gifted math students are flexible in their approach to practiced solutions and can readjust when they fail.[10] Think, for example, of the episode in the film *Hidden Figures* about the African American women who, in the days before mechanical computers, were hired as human computers to track the trajectory of early manned spacecraft. When things start to go wrong, the main protagonist in the film, Katherine Johnson, convinces her colleagues to abandon the usual method of calculating and try a much older one, the Euler method. It works and the spacecraft, along with its astronaut, John Glenn, lands in the predicted spot in the ocean. While the plot is truly gripping, and the film tells an important story about the unrecognized African American women behind the early space program, the scene is also important because it rubs against a common image of math as cut and dried, and it shows how disciplined experience is tightly tied to real-life events and strong human emotions.

True, Johnson did not have much room for error, and once she and her colleagues selected the Euler method, they still had a lot of exact calculation to do. While most of the computing would be done by machine (not human) computers today, the episode demonstrates the important role cognitive flexibility plays in inquiry. And flexibility involves the recognition of mistakes and a willingness to consider alternative possibilities.

While students gifted in mathematics are reported to be flexible in the way they approach problems, flexibility is not often included as one of the aims of general math education. But this is likely more because of the pressure teachers feel to get through the syllabus than to the ability of students to understand what they are doing and why.

---

[10] Hersh and John-Steiner, *Loving and Hating Mathematics*, p. 24.

Teaching students to be flexible in their approach to problem solving would require that teachers probe a student's comprehension, so both teacher and student could understand the reason for the student's response. One of the marks of truly good teaching is the ability to probe the mistakes of students and to sense the kinds of steps needed to correct them. Of course this requires that teachers have a strong grasp of mathematics and of how to follow a student's thought process. This is true not only for lessons in math but also for lessons in democracy.

TAKING MISTAKES SERIOUSLY

Recognizing mistakes can play a critical role in shaping a democratic character, but their value depends on the way they are treated. Simply correcting a mistake has limited value. Had Mrs. Perry taught us the old saw, "Ours is not to reason why, just invert and multiply," she would have provided a cute, helpful, mnemonic device but she would have added little to my understanding.

Reflection calls for an analysis of "blunders" and of the logic that led to them. The aim of reflection is more than just helping the student produce the right answer. It is also to help the student see the reason for the misunderstanding. A closer look at my blunder and the logic behind it will help illustrate this point. Mistakes can be useful in defining the scope of a rule, and in understanding a problem better. Understanding the scope of a rule is critical for math, as well as for democracy.

As noted previously, my problem in dividing fractions was that I inappropriately extended the scope of the rules I had learned about the process on normal division, and as a result, I did not fully grasp what it meant to divide a fraction by a fraction. I did not see that I was being asked about the composition of a *half* (i.e., how many quarters can go into it, or how many quarters does it take to make a half). The answer "2" was confusing because I was taking it to mean two wholes, which is in fact larger than either ½ or ¼. Had I realized that the 2 does not refer to the whole but to fractions of a whole, namely quarters – an exercise that I frequently performed whenever I exchanged a half dollar for two quarters – then the answer would have made sense and would have been consistent with my prevailing idea of the way division is supposed to behave.

THE POTENTIAL OF MATH TO ESTABLISH AN INFORMED RELATIONSHIP TO RULES

Math has the potential to provide unique opportunities to reflect on rules and the purposes they serve. It can make students aware of the possible interconnectedness of the various parts of a subject, as well as connections between one subject field and others. When students learn to make connections, they are less likely to be buffeted by unexpected events. They have a better understanding of how some events serve as sign of others and are more likely to address them productively. In its very abstractness, math can alert students to the formation of different patterns of relationships in preparation for a more content-dependent experience that they will encounter in other courses, such as history or science. It also has the potential for teachers to treat students as more than simply answering machines in training that get it either right or wrong.

SEEKING CONNECTIONS

The math educator, Liping Ma, distinguishes three different levels of math knowledge: (1) The procedural level, or knowing how to follow an algorithm – like invert and multiply. (2) The conceptual level, or understanding how the algorithm actually works and what you are doing when you follow it. (3) The relational level, or understanding the connections between different operations, like borrowing in addition, and stacking numbers like a staircase when multiplying more than single digit numbers.[11]

I was stuck at the procedural level in Mrs. Perry's class because I did not fully understand what was going on at the conceptual level

---

[11] Ma, *Knowing and Teaching Elementary Mathematics*, pp. 118–122.

when asked to divide a fraction by a fraction. Nor did I see how this procedure was connected to other procedures. Understanding the principle behind these procedures could have provided a useful map that could help navigate later math. As Ma notes,

> Approaching a topic in various ways, making an argument for various solutions, comparing the solutions and finding a best one, in fact, is a constant force in the development of mathematics. An advanced operation or advanced branch in mathematics usually offers a more sophisticated way to solve problems. Multiplication, for example, is a more sophisticated operation than addition for solving some problems. Algebraic methods of solving problems are more sophisticated than arithmetical ones. When a problem is solved in multiple ways, it serves as a tie connecting several pieces of mathematical knowledge.[12]

To teach math for democracy's sake is not to water it down but to go both deeper and broader, perhaps slower. The aim is both a better, more flexible understanding of how math works and a better, more flexible understanding of how rules work. "This allows for a sophisticated and coherent picture of elementary mathematics ... that elementary mathematics is not a simple collection of disconnected number facts and calculational algorithms,"[13] and it can provide the basis for productive discussion and even debate without the sense that the loudest voice or the cleverest rhetorical strategy will inevitably win.

CYNICISM AND MYSTIFICATION: ANTIDEMOCRATIC POSSIBILITIES

Ironically while mathematics is largely viewed as the foundation of rational thought, it is not often viewed as much use for rational discussion. One reason for this disparity is traced to the view of math as advanced by Plato: a realm of certainty available to only a

---

[12] Ibid., p. 112.   [13] Ibid., p. 116.

few exceptional human beings but largely unavailable to the rest of us.[14] Plato held that mathematics represented a pure form of knowledge, accessible to only a few, and that the best society would be governed by those few people able to achieve insight into those forms. As the philosopher Karl Popper pointed out, this not only serves to justify the closed, totalitarian society but also provides an ideal and unforgiving conception of the intellectual background for trust formation.[15] The failure of government to reach perfection serves, ironically, as a breeding ground for cynicism to develop and for the world in which real humans live to be taken as forever defective. As Dewey writes of Plato's philosophy:

> For they brought with them the idea of a higher realm of fixed reality of which alone true science is possible and of an inferior world of changing things with which experience and practical matters are concerned. They glorified the invariant at the expense of change, it being evident that all practical activity falls within the realm of change. It bequeathed the notion which has ruled philosophy ever since the time of the Greeks, that the office of knowledge is to uncover the antecedently real, rather than, as is the case with our practical judgment, to gain the kind of understanding which is necessary to deal with problems as they arise.[16]

While the Platonic view allows for the possibility of "real" knowledge, even if only among the very few, a modern view places doubt on the unquestionable character of mathematical knowledge, holding that the very basis of math, the axioms upon which theorems are built, are themselves assumed to be true without proof and that many basic terms go undefined.[17] Given this understanding of mathematics,

[14] *The Republic of Plato*, Francis Cornford, tr. (Oxford: Oxford University Press, 1945).

[15] Karl Popper, *The Open Society and Its Enemies* (Princeton: Princeton University Press, 1945/2013).

[16] John Dewey, *The Quest for Certainty* (New York: Capricorn Books, 1960) p. 16.

[17] Michael Meyerson, *Political Numeracy: Mathematical Perspective on Our Changing Constitution* (New York: Norton, 2002), p. 24.

cynicism can find even more support. If the foundation of even mathematical claims is shaky, then how can any truth claim be trusted?

Cynicism is the converse of trust. It is the view that the basic ideals and principles of a society are inherently deceptive, empty, unprovable slogans, inevitably used to conceal exploitation of the many by the few. A practical response to unquestioned cynicism is to join the exploiters whenever possible or passively accept despair when it is not.

DISTINCTION BETWEEN CYNICISM AND SKEPTICISM AND BETWEEN CYNICISM AND RELATIVISM

The cynic questions both the possibility of truth itself and the global intentions of anyone trying to convince another person that some claim is true. While cynics reject even the possibility of any and all truth, skeptics question the validity of only a specific claim to truth. Skepticism and doubt are conditions of inquiry. Cynicism is the denial of its possibility.

Cynicism is self-reinforcing. It contributes to exploitation of others by promoting a sense of global helplessness and inevitable victimhood. It licenses abuse of the weak by the strong through the presumption that everyone except naïve fools will steal and lie when they believe they can get away with it. The cynic rejects the very idea of a common good[18] as either a ploy of the rich and powerful or a fantasy of the weak and poor.

If cynicism is generalized, then everyone seeks to maximize their own private benefit, with the aim of joining the "self-serving" wealthy and powerful, while disadvantaging even further those who refuse to do so. When generalized, one person's selfish behavior communicates to everyone else that selfishness is the only prudent way to behave. Society then becomes a zero-sum game where everyone

---

[18] Philip H. Phenix, *Education and the Common Good: A Moral Philosophy of the Curriculum* (New York: Harper & Brothers, 1961). See also Michael Sandel, *The Tyranny of Merit: What's Become of the Common Good?* (New York: Farrar, Straus and Giroux, 2020).

strives to be a freeloader, with the result that all are worse off than they would be if people believed in the existence of a common good.

This is one of those cases where belief creates the reality. Cynicism is a strong weight against the formation of a coherent body of citizens working together to advance a shared approach to the common good.

Of course Platonism is still preserved in high places without cynicism, as the renowned mathematician G. H. Hardy reports:

> I believe that mathematical reality lies outside of us, that our function is to discover or *observe* it, and that the theorems which we prove, and which we describe grandiloquently as our "creations" are simply our notes of our observations.[19]

Or, with a strong dose of removal and austerity,

> The mass of mathematical truth is obvious and imposing; its practical applications, the bridges and steam engines and dynamos, obtrude themselves on the dullest imagination ... Mathematicians must feel that it is not on these *crude* achievements that the real case for mathematics rest.[20]

In any case the Platonic view either mystifies mathematics without any answer to the question, how will we know the philosopher king when he appears, or it affects indifference to the earthly concerns of mere mortals.

MYSTIFICATION AS THE OTHER SIDE OF CYNICISM

Mystification is the other side of cynicism. Both involve a rejection of the ability of truth claims to be publicly and rationally assessed. The difference is that, while the cynic holds that any failure is the result of conscious cunning and power, the mystified person attributes the

---

[19] G. H. Hardy, *A Mathematician's Apology* (Cambridge: Cambridge University Press, electronic ed., 1967), p. 196 of 244.
[20] Ibid., p. 103 (italics mine).

failure to his own incapacity to comprehend. The cynic trusts his own intuitions completely and rejects anything that contradicts them, largely because he rejects any claim to reason or to ethical motivation; the mystified distrusts his own intuition completely and seeks external validation before coming to his "own" conclusions. The mystified does not deny the possibility of truth, as does the cynic; he only questions his own capability to grasp it. In his blind trust, the mystified is willing to follow any charismatic leader. Mystification in the classroom is encouraged when students are taught to ignore their own understanding in order to please the teacher and to obey her authority in pursuit of the right answer. The consequences of mystification – loss of voice, discretion, and agency – can be a primary motor for authoritarian regimes and is as serious threat to the fate of democracy, as the retreat into cynicism.

BRINGING MATHEMATICS DOWN TO EARTH

Dewey's instrumental view of math is a viable alternative to the Platonic view. He dismisses the Platonic vision of truth with the apt label "the quest for certainty," which he rightly views as futile and unproductive. For Dewey, mathematics is a part of inquiry, and all genuine inquiry has an open-ended quality about it. Hence, the fact that some terms go undefined and axioms unproved is of little concern. What is important is their fruits.

> For centuries, the axioms and definitions of Euclidean geometry
> were regarded as absolute first principles which could be accepted
> without question. Preoccupation with a new order of problems
> disclosed that they were both overlapping and deficient as logical
> grounds for a generalized geometry. The result has made it clear
> that instead of being "self-evident" truths immediately known,
> they are postulates adopted because of what follow from them.[21]

---

[21] John Dewey, *Logic: The Theory of Inquiry* (New York: Henry Holt and Company, 1938), p. 141.

Accounting for the apparent rigor of mathematics, the mathematician Reuben Hersh makes a similar point:

> [L]ofty rigor is not found in all mathematics. From one specialty to another, from one mathematician to another, there's variation in strictness of proof and applicability of results.
>
> In developing and understanding a subject, axioms come late. Then in the formal presentation they come early.
>
> The view that mathematics is in essence derivations from axioms is backward. In fact it is wrong.[22]

The openness of the mathematical process is quite different from the way in which mathematics is often presented by schools, as a unique subject requiring a special and innate talent, hence giving math courses their special status, while obscuring ways in which mathematics can serve to nurture democratic culture and character. In contrast, for Dewey what gives mathematics its special character is not some mystical quality, but the fact that it is abstracted from any existential item (e.g., two quarters make a half dollar) and that the objects of math have meaning only in relation to one another. There is a benefit to abstraction of course. It can be applied to any and all objects, but this benefit is better served when students can have a concrete understanding of what they are expected to do.

For example, money in the form of some token and counting may have first developed to make easier transfer of, say, part of the fall wheat crop for ten new lambs in the spring. Instead of carting wheat one place and herding lambs to another, a value is set and a coin invented, and it is agreed to establish that coin as having a certain value that represents the equivalent value of the wheat and the lamb. Where the wheat and the lamb are both valued the same in clay tokens, say thirty, that can be satisfied in many ways (e.g., one 30-ounce coin, one 5- and one 25-ounce coin, etc.). Once the numbers are

---

[22] Reuben Hersh, *What Is Mathematics Really?* (New York: Oxford University Press, 1997), p. 6.

invented and tied to specific objects, they can be abstracted – or removed from that tie – and applied to any other object, along with certain rules of transferability (e.g., 20 + 10 = 25 + 5). The important things from the instrumentalist view are that the math is grounded in existential reality and that it can be abstracted from that particular reality and then applied to other existential concerns. It is true that as rules of transferability become more complicated, people like Hardy will develop an interest in the implication of the rules themselves, somewhat like the craft person may become less interested in using tools and more interested in refining them and inventing new and even more beautiful ones. But the fact that math can become an interest in its own right should not obscure the role it has in opening up real-world possibilities of improving our capacity to both engage and enjoy the world in which we find ourselves, and in this way, it can be harnessed to serve democratic thought and culture.

MORE THAN CALCULATION

Calculation will always be a part of math, but most mathematicians today view calculation as but a small piece of the larger field, which they define somewhat elusively as the science of abstract patterns.[23] Keith Devlin reports that historically identifying math as the study of numbers is a very early conception of mathematics, followed by a later focus on geometry, and then much later, calculus or the study of motion and change was added.[24] Today the subfields of math number in the thousands, and as a result, the definition of math has shifted to the now preferred science of patterns.[25] The subjects vary from number theory, the study of patterns of numbers; to geometry, the study of patterns of shapes; to calculus, the study of patterns of motion; to logic, the study of patterns of reasoning; to probability, the study of patterns of chance; to topography, studies of closeness

---

[23] Keith Devlin, *Mathematics: The Science of Patterns* (New York: Scientific American Library, 1997), p. 3.
[24] Ibid., pp. 1–2.   [25] Ibid., p. 3.

and position;[26] and many more. As the study of patterns, mathematics is concerned with the way things are related or "the structures in which they are arranged."[27]

One effect of broadening the definition of math is to allow for new ways of thinking about thinking and about the nature of certainty. For example, when the weather forecaster tells me that there is a 60 percent chance of rain, his calculation may be indubitable, in that under similar weather conditions, it has rained 60 percent of the time, but this certainty does not tell me whether to carry an umbrella to work or not.

To view math as the science of patterns broadens the conception of school math, allowing logic and statistics to be included as math. It also highlights the potential relevance of mathematical instruments to other areas of the curriculum. Consider, as an example, the way in which political geometry can be used to open up questions about the relative weight of individual votes in different districts for social studies classes. The difference between arithmetic and exponential growth in addressing contemporary problems, such as tracking pandemics in health or science classes or calculating rates of global warming in earth science courses.

THE ROLE OF MATHEMATICS IN DISCIPLINING EXPERIENCE

A number of years ago, I was observing an eighth-grade manual training class. Sally finished making a tray, and another student praised her work. Sally responded, "Thank you, but it needs a lot of work. Look at how the corners don't fit together very well. I need to learn how to measure more precisely before I try to build another one."

---

[26] Ibid.

[27] Michael M. Fried, "Mathematics as the Science of Patterns," *Convergence*, August 2010 (online); available at www.maa.org/press/periodicals/convergence/mathematics-as-the-science-of-patterns-mathematics-as-the-science-of-patterns#:~:text=The%25.

Sally makes a natural connection between the quality of her work – the tray – and the activity of using numbers and measuring. In the process, she has also gained an understanding of the need for precision and a sense of how she might achieve it.[28] And, most importantly, she has appealed to an abstract standard to help her judge the quality of her work. She was developing the ability to look at her own work dispassionately and to judge it against some objective and communicative standard, while at the same time inviting her classmate to use that same standard to evaluate her work.

The fact that all of this did not just take place in Sally's head, but rather as she engaged in a process of communication with others, is a critical factor in the formation of a democratic citizenry. Precision, self-reflection, and self-correction by themselves are valuable qualities to have in their own right; in setting communal standards, they can also aid in shaping collective judgment, whether in constructing a tray or monitoring an environment.

A concern for precision should be one of the great benefits of math education, but the quest for precision is often mistaken for the quest for the right answer. A fixation with the right answer can obscure the fact that mathematics is a tool that is useful for identifying and addressing certain kinds of problems. This fixation can reinforce an authoritarian relationship, where the student looks to the teacher for validation, ignoring other ideas and dismissing them as "mere opinions." Moreover, while there are some places where this kind of hierarchical relationship has a role to play – say, master to apprentice – rising citizens need other models of authority as well, just as they need an alternative understanding of precision. This is a topic for the next chapter.

---

[28] There is some issue among educational researchers about the transfer of learning from one field to another (Thorndike). However, this example is largely meant to be hypothetical and does not claim to support or contradict that research. The point is that something about precision is being learned without any claim to how far it is extended.

7 STEM and the Democratic Aims of Science Education

In some imaginary world, run by a benign, all-knowing, all-benevolent dictator, all laws and regulations would be reasonable, and everyone would follow them. In a pandemic, everyone would be vaccinated; in a dangerously warming world, everyone would be mobilized to cool it; in a world where waste threatens ocean life, new regulations limiting the use and disposal of plastics would be promoted and followed universally.

But democracies do not work this way. There is no benign dictator. Instead, there are groups of citizens from different backgrounds, with different interests and affiliations, who together, or through their representatives, must arrive at a workable consensus. To reach this consensus, citizens need also to believe that their efforts to hold the line will not be in vain. If I cannot depend on you to wear a mask, when mask wearing has proven to be effective protection; to adjust your thermostat downward; to dispose of your waste in an appropriate way, then my incentive for doing the same is reduced. Citizens need to have confidence in the long-term projections of science, and each individual needs to trust that they will not be alone in acting on these projections. The recent resistance to reasonable warnings about global warming, the spread of pandemics, and the threat to the global food supply suggest this is not an easy thing to do.

A major aim of science education for custodians of democracy then should be to develop and promote the basic habits required to protect the institutional production, application, and dissemination of reliable knowledge.[1] This chapter examines the implications of this

---

[1] This aim is not meant to replace the need for scientific literacy, but rather to extend the notion of literacy to include the institutional structures in which knowledge

aim for the education of the rising citizen, including future scientists and engineers.

THE THALIDOMIDE EPISODE: A MODEL
OF SUCCESSFUL INSTITUTIONALIZATION

In 1957, a new, over-the-counter drug, thalidomide, entered the European market as a safe, effective remedy for morning sickness and as a sleep aid. The drug was widely used in Europe and was awaiting Food and Drug Administration (FDA) approval in the United States. Given the size of the US market, pharmaceutical companies had a special interest in its approval, and in the early 1960s, considerable pressure was exerted by the drug company, Richardson-Merrell, on a young FDA inspector, Dr. Frances Kelsey, who was in charge of the approval process. Despite this pressure, Kelsey held up approval because she was concerned that the drug had not been adequately tested.

Trained as both a pharmacologist and a physician, Kelsey had recently learned that some drugs could pass through the placenta barrier, potentially damaging the fetus, and she wanted more data before recommending approval.

Meanwhile, in Australia, a medical doctor, William McBride, began to notice that a number of infants, whose mothers had taken the drug, were born with shriveled limbs, and he reported a possible connection between the drug and the birth defect. The connection was not easy to detect because the effects of the drug on the fetus occurred only if it was taken between the fourth and eighth weeks of pregnancy. It is estimated that over 100,000 babies worldwide were formed with stunted limbs, but thanks to Kelsey, most of the

claims are produced, tested, validated, and disseminated. Nor is this aim meant as a substitute for the training required to meet the need for specialized scientists and professionals. However, as I will show, it does add an additional dimension to their education. Rather the aim is meant to address the need for citizens to maintain control over a process that has ever-increasing consequences for the way they live their lives at a time when this process is becoming ever more complex.

newborns in the United States were spared this devastating condition. Besides saving many thousands of families from great grief, Kelsey's work also resulted in the Kefauver–Harris Amendment, which mandated more rigorous drug testing.

The story does not quite end there. Building on previous research, and over sixty years after the ban on thalidomide, newer research revealed the chemical mechanism by which the drug penetrated the placenta wall, thus causing the defect. Understanding the causal mechanism and limiting its use, researchers today have begun to find other applications for the drug in treating a wide range of medical conditions, including leprosy, myeloma, cancers, and HIV, among others.[2] The long history of thalidomide reveals a neglected feature of contemporary science education – the workings of an open-ended community of scientists extended in both time and space. Given this neglect, students are likely to leave school with a one-sided, heroic understanding of science, as the achievements of single individuals working alone to uncover the secrets of nature. This needs to be corrected, and students need a more accurate understanding of the workings of the scientific community and of the roles it will play in their futures as both producers and consumers of scientific knowledge and technological innovations.

Science Education for Rising Citizens

Presently two aims dominate science education: First, familiarity with basic scientific facts – scientific literacy; second, to provide students with practical laboratory or field experience. The thalidomide example highlights a neglected third – to acquaint students with the working of the larger scientific community as a community. This aim has implications for the work of both those who will be directly involved in the production of scientific knowledge and technological

[2] Dana-Farber Cancer Institute, "After 60 Years Scientists Uncovered How Thalidomide Produced Birth Defects," *News Releases*, August 1, 2018 (online); available at www.dana-farber.org/newsroom/news-releases/2018/after-60-years-scientists-uncover-how-thalidomide-produced-birth-defects/.

innovation and for those citizens who, while not involved directly in the production of scientific knowledge, will be consumers of scientific and technological innovation. For the producers of scientific knowledge and innovation, the aim calls for improving communication across disciplinary boundaries. For the consumers, it calls for understanding the way in which science is used and misused to justify claims to legitimacy.

Democratic Values in Science

Schools largely separate courses in science from civics or courses in democracy. This is understandable given the prevailing philosophy that separates facts from values, but this philosophy captures only the superficial side of the story and has been significantly challenged by philosophers like Hilary Putnam[3] and others. I don't want to rehearse the technical arguments here[4] except to note that the view that they are separate assumes the heroic individualistic image of science while neglecting the communal side. In what follows, I bring the communal aspect of science back into focus to show how democratic values can serve to productively infiltrate science and technology. I begin with a well-known episode of technology gone wrong – the *Challenger* Tragedy.

The Role of Communicative Distortion in the Challenger Disaster

On January 28, 1986, on a cold clear day, as I, along with millions of others, watched on television, the signal for takeoff was given at Cape Canaveral, Florida, to the crew of the *Challenger* space shuttle. On board was a high-school teacher, Christa McAuliffe, from Concord, New Hampshire. Her presence was to serve as an iconic example, marking the progress of science and engineering in the twentieth century.

---

[3] Hilary Putnam, *The Collapse of the Fact/Value Dichotomy and Other Essays* (Cambridge: Harvard University Press, 2002), 1–68.

[4] See also Walter Feinberg, "Critical Pragmatism and the Reconnection of Science and Values in Educational Research," *European Journal of American Philosophy and Pragmatism* IV(1) (2012) (online); available at http://journala.openedition.org/ejpap/786.

McAuliffe had been selected from over 11,000 applicants to be the first teacher in space. While on board the spacecraft, she was expected to perform experiments and to teach lessons that would be televised back to classrooms on earth. Her selection, the result of a decision by the Reagan administration to popularize the space program and to encourage more students to be interested in science, was consistent with her own teaching about the importance of ordinary people in making history. Sadly, none of this was to come to pass. Seventy-three seconds into the flight and 48,000 feet above the earth's surface, the *Challenger* exploded, killing her and everyone else aboard. The planned celebration quickly turned into a scene of horror and a day of mourning.

Many people saw this as a failure of technology, narrowly understood. Something must have gone wrong with the many complicated calculations required to set a spacecraft aloft or to land it safely. With the wrong calculation, the craft could tumble back to earth or, even worse, skim over the earth's atmosphere, hurling it and everyone aboard into outer space forever, never to return. Few of us knew exactly how these calculations worked, but we marveled at the scientific and engineering skills that had made most previous space endeavors safe and successful.

But not this one. What could have gone wrong? What error in calculation had resulted in this national catastrophe? The problem, as we will see, was not with "the rocket science," a term that along with "brain surgery" has come to signal the most complex of problem-solving tasks. Indeed, the failure was not with the science at all, at least not the commonly understood heroic conception of science, but with a breakdown in the habits of democracy and communication within a scientific community.

BEYOND ROCKET SCIENCE

The tragedy was avoidable. The *Challenger* was not some newfangled ship. Prior to the disaster, it had flown in numerous separate missions for a total of sixty-two days. Rather, the explosion was the result of a simple and correctable glitch. Flight Control had only to wait a few days for the weather to warm, and the problem would correct itself. The technical part of the failure was the result of inflammable gases passing through the O-rings, which had shrunk in size temporarily as a result of unusually cold weather.

But the O-rings were only a tiny part of this huge project. Compared to the sophisticated computers, the advance electronics, and the state-of-the-art technology, O-rings have little claim to fame. You can find them in your kitchen sink and in your car engine. They are basically a small, flexible gasket that seals different compartments of hard tubes or pipes together. They provide both flexibility and security and have probably been around since the invention of pipes. You can buy them at any hardware or home supply store. Likely, the O-rings for the *Challenger* were made of special material and fitted with more precision than your everyday O-ring, but, nevertheless, they were simply O-rings. Yet it was the failure of this simple, ordinary part that blew a multimillion-dollar machine apart, wiping out the lives of all seven people aboard.

Technical knowledge was not the issue. Again, with all these technical advances, the accident could have been averted. Someone could have predicted that the O-rings might fail. And, in fact, someone did. The engineers on the project anticipated failure and warned against launch. So why was the launch given the go-ahead? The answer has a lot to do with simple communication in a situation of unequal power and rhetorical intimidation.

GO OR NO-GO

One of the engineers on the project, Roger M. Boisjoly, has provided a riveting description of the negotiations that went on before the launch.[5] Months prior to launch, Boisjoly had reported a number of problems that he had found with the O-rings, and he had expressed

---

[5] Roger M. Boisjoly, "The *Challenger* Disaster: Moral Responsibility and the Working Engineer," Copyright by Roger M. Boisjoly, 1987.

concern to his supervisors that lower than usual temperatures could result in the unwanted blowback of hot gases. The data was discussed with the company (Morton Thiokol) management "but thought too sensitive by them to release."[6] Still, everyone on the project became aware of the danger at a meeting held on July 1, 1985, and an urgent memo was reportedly sent out on August 15, 1985, at 2:30 p.m., with the conclusion, "It is my honest and very real fear that if we do not take immediate action to dedicate a team to solve the problem, with the field joint having the number one priority, then we stand in jeopardy of losing a flight."[7]

But NASA management instructed the engineers "not to express the critical urgency of fixing the joint."[8] The day before the launch, the temperature dipped to 18 degrees Fahrenheit, well below what the engineers considered safe for the launch. A warning went out, and the engineers, whose approval was required for the launch to take place, recommended not to launch below 53 degrees. NASA management was not happy with the recommendation, arguing that the data was inconclusive, and at one point the chief manager turned to the head engineer, who had ultimate authority to postpone the launch, and told him to take off his engineering hat and put on his management hat; the decision to launch was approved.

LESSON FOR CUSTODIANS OF DEMOCRACY

What can this event and others like it tell us about the requirements of science education when citizens serve the dual role of professional expert and custodians of democracy? Obviously, a society does not need to be democratic to launch rockets successfully. Germany, under the Nazis, did it quite well, although it is unlikely that any failure, especially one as monumental as the *Challenger*, would have been publicized.

Publicity is both a disadvantage (because it can slow things down) and an advantage (because it can slow things down). In fact,

---

[6] Ibid., p. 7.   [7] Ibid., p. 8.   [8] Ibid.

in a democracy it is *supposed* to slow things down by being a part of a complex feedback mechanism that allows citizens to understand and give their voice to the value of the project. This feedback mechanism is at the heart of political democracy, and its failure provides an object lesson for rising citizens. But in this case the failure of *political* democracy was not the primary cause of the explosion. Rather it was a failure in *cultural* democracy, that is, tonal intimidation from bureaucratic authority.

To see the failure in cultural democracy, let us look closely at the interaction between the engineers and the managers before the launch and at the way intimidation was communicated through the tone of the discourse. As I noted earlier, the engineers got their technical science right, but there was more to the *science* than the physics of the O-ring.

Let's return to Boisjoly's description of events, starting after tests showed the vulnerability of the O-rings.

1. "This data was discussed with Morton Thiokol engineering management but was thought to be too sensitive for them to release" (p. 7).

2. "However, I was given strict instructions, which came from NASA, not to express the critical urgency of fixing the joint but to only emphasize the joint improvement aspect during my presentation" (p. 8).

3. "The evening meeting of Jan. 27, 1986 was the concluding event preceding the launch disaster. The major activity that day focused upon the predicted 18 degrees Fahrenheit overnight temperature and meeting with engineering management to persuade them not to launch. ... The teleconference with KSC (Kennedy Space Center) and MSFC (Marshall Space Flight Center) started with a history of O-ring damage in field points. Data was presented showing a major concern with seal resiliency and the change to the sealing timing function and the criticality of this on the ability to seal. I was asked several times during our portion of the presentation to qualify my concerns but I said I could not since the only data I had was what I had presented and that I had been trying to get more data since last October. At this comment, the general manager of Morton Thiokol gave a scolding look as if to say, 'Why are you telling that to them!'" (p. 8).

4. "Our General Manager ... said in a soft voice 'We have to make a management decision.' I became furious when I heard this because I know that an attempt would be made by management to reverse our recommendation" (p. 9).

5. "Arnie stopped [trying to explain our position] when he saw the unfriendly look in Mason's eyes and also realized that no one was listening to him. I then grabbed the photographic evidence showing the hot gas blow-by ... and admonished them to look at it ... I too received the same cold stares as Arnie with looks as if to say 'go away and don't bother us with the facts.' At that moment I felt totally helpless and further argument was fruitless so I, too, stopped pressing my case" (p. 9).

6. "Then Mason turned to Bob Lund, the vice-president of engineering, and told him to take off his engineering hat and put on his management hat" (p. 9).

And so he did, and, as a result, the launch took place, and the *Challenger* exploded. Again, the launch failed, not because of any collapse of the technical knowledge required by rocket science – everyone knew almost everything that needed to be known – but because in the rush to accomplish bureaucratic goals, professional knowledge was silenced, its significance consciously distorted and then ignored.

LESSONS FOR THE EDUCATION OF CUSTODIANS:
AN ANALYSIS OF A DYSFUNCTIONAL CULTURE

Boisjoly's list raises scientific and educational issues. For example, items 1 and 2 raise ethical questions about scientific production and who has a right to keep critical information secret. And it raises questions about when and if it is justified to do so. Item 3 not only addresses the technical concern but also describes the interpersonal communicative dynamics and the pressure that the engineers were subjected to. Items 4 and 5 indicate that the bullying behavior was eventually successful and that the decision to launch was not made on technical grounds but as a result of power within the organization's production process. Item 6 highlights the perception of the competing interests involved in the negotiation, the rhetorical steps used to align them, and the way in which a subordinate priority – a timely launch – came to trump a more critical one: the safety of the crew.

Together they suggest that science education is much more than strictly vocational in the narrow sense of the term. Scientists, as much as any other citizen, need to be critically aware of the values and the communicative environment in which they function. So, in speaking of the education of scientists, we should also be speaking of the education of scientists as citizens who may also serve as custodians of democracy.

LESSON FOR FUTURE CUSTODIANS: LEARN HOW TO SPEAK TO AUTHORITY

Suppose we could go back in time and replay the scenes. Suppose that Lund had said to Mason, "Well, yes, I have put on my manager's hat, and I have decided that the cost to the country would be far greater from a catastrophic accident than from simply another delay, and, if necessary, I will explain to the politicians and the public why it is necessary to wait for warmer weather." Here the engineer as citizen trumps the engineer as management, but it is his expertise as an engineer that lends credibility to this trump card. The engineer is given veto power because, as an expert, he is acting in the name of the civic authority to place safety above cost effectiveness. And when acting in their name, he is acting as citizen as well as engineer.

Yet Lund was not fully prepared to exert this civilian authority and to take on his role as a *citizen* representative of the nation's best interest. Had he been so prepared, he might have said that while he appreciated the intensity of the management's feelings, and the pressures they were under to save money and avoid still another delay, the engineers cannot be bullied by collective silence, or by scolding, or even by patronizing irrelevant exhortations. The engineer/citizen cannot approve the launch until the weather changes, or the O-rings are tested further.

Of course, many of us have been placed in the same kind of uncomfortable situation as Lund, and many, myself included, have failed at one point or another – although hopefully without the same level of dire consequences. Yet it certainly helps to address these situations by being prepared educationally for them. The educational goal for rising citizens as custodians is to learn to be properly cautious but without being paralyzed. This requires proving space for alternative opinions to be heard and to become aware of extraneous or rhetoric devises to muffle them.

THE *CHALLENGER* AS AN EDUCATIONAL FAILURE

Boisjoly's account illustrates the dual role that engineers play in the system, as both highly technical experts and as citizens responsible to communicate the results of their expertise to those who are not experts. In the dual capacity as engineers and citizens, they need to be able to coordinate the various parts of the project toward the goal (e.g., a safe flight). As citizens, they also need to set the conditions for smooth communication between the different parts of the system with one another, and of the project as a whole, with the general public.

BUT IS IT SCIENCE?

The work of science is informed by values at virtually every stage, from the problem that is selected for study, to the way a problem is defined, and from the methods chosen to test a claim, to definitions that delineate the object to be investigated. Science also underscores the logic that moves the argument from premise to conclusion and from logical conclusion to the process by which the results are published – first in the scientific literature and then in the popular press – or, as in the case of the *Challenger*, to action.

The everyday work of scientists is informed by value concerns at many different levels. It is somewhat arbitrary to decide just what part of this work is to be called "real science" and to then restrict that to the phase of data collection, experimentation, and explanation, while bracketing anything having to do with values as nonscientific. Scientific knowledge, in the narrow technical sense, impacts strongly upon values. Perhaps the most striking example is the impact of scientific knowledge upon the system of values promulgated by the church during the Middle Ages. "That system rested upon a credo about the nature of the universe, its creator, and man's connection to that creator ... The new approach is based upon radically different concepts, and leads to a radically different conception of both the universe and man's place in the universe."[9] The idea that values are implicated at the deepest level even in the physical sciences should give pause to the idea that the boundaries between science and values are absolute and impermeable.[10]

The education for custodians needs to develop an awareness of the mutual infiltration of facts and values, while providing the ability to expose and interrogate the value implications of both the claims that scientists make and the process used to make and support them. As Hilary Putnam puts it: "[I]nquiry is a cooperative human interaction with an environment; and both aspects, the active intervention, the active manipulation of the environment, and the cooperation of other human beings are vital."[11]

CALIBRATING EPISTEMIC EXPECTATIONS

Protecting the process of inquiry requires realistic expectations regarding the stability of scientific knowledge. One of the perceived differences between the natural sciences and the social sciences is the duration of their findings. On average, the findings of the natural sciences, including mathematics, tend to endure longer and to apply more generally than the findings of the social sciences. So, Newton's laws will have more staying power than, say, the claims about racial differences in intelligence based on IQ test scores.[12]

---

[9] Henry P. Stapp, "Quantum Physics and Human Values," *Science and Culture in the 21st Century-Agenda for Survival*, UNESCO, September 22, 1989 (online); available at https://escholarship.org/uc/item/47p3r51m.

[10] Feinberg, "Critical Pragmatism and the Reconnection of Science and Values in Educational Research."

[11] Hilary Putnam, *Pragmatism* (Oxford: Blackwell, 1995), p. 70.

[12] Feinberg, *Understanding Education*.

When creationists dismiss evolution as "only a theory," they not only exhibit a uniformed understanding of the nature of science but also display a critical miscalculation regarding appropriate epistemic expectations. "Only a theory" implies that real knowledge must be unchanging, but science just doesn't work that way. True, some knowledge claims have remarkable stability. Archimedes' law of the lever still works for most things after a couple of millennia of trials. And others not so much – the phlogiston theory, for example, has now been relegated to the ever-growing trash heap of scientific dead ends. It was, indeed, *only* a theory.

While few can predict with a high degree of accuracy whether a new finding will have the staying power of the law of levers or join phlogiston on the trash heap of science, they can begin to understand the processes that are involved in promoting one idea or demoting another. Certainly, evolution comes closer to the law of levers than to phlogiston in its stability – but then, of course, there is always that remote possibility. The important point for the education of custodians of democracy is that expectations regarding the stability of scientific knowledge need to be appropriately calibrated to fit the nature of the inquiry itself if scientific inquiry is to be adequately protected.

Certainly, science can be a contact sport and even the best of scientists can differ fiercely over data and its meaning. From the outside, this can be frustrating – one study says this, but another says that – what's a person to believe? To the absolutists, those who hold that knowledge claims are either right or wrong, or to those who have miscalibrated conceptions of the stability of knowledge, this indecision will look like a fatal flaw, one that discredits science as a whole. In fact, however, the failure of science to come up with absolutes is part of the very strength of science, and it is essential to its capacity for self-correction. But miscalibration can influence the ability of people to respond to reasonably reliable knowledge claims.

Science education for rising citizens involves an understanding of the ways in which science generates knowledge claims and the

factors that influence it. Take as an example the long-standing issue –
now settled – whether cigarettes are a cause of cancer. They are.

WHAT'S A CITIZEN TO DO WHEN SCIENTIFIC CLAIMS CONFLICT?

The long failure to fully understand the influence of smoking on
cancer was the result of interaction by a number of factors. First,
before other diseases (e.g., tuberculosis, typhus) were tamed, cancer
was not recognized as a major threat, and so science largely ignored it.
This was understandable given that these other diseases killed off
many people in the prime of their lives, well before many were old
enough to get cigarette-caused cancer. But even after deaths from
these other diseases were significantly reduced, and the correlation
between smoking and cancer became obvious, cigarette companies
continued to deny that there was a causal relationship. They *argued,
correctly,* that the exact chemical responsible for cancer was uncertain, but in doing so they focused attention away from the question
"do cigarettes cause cancer?" to the question "what is the chemical
that causes cancer?" And then there was a legitimate scientific dis-
pute – rarely brought to the public attention – regarding the competing scientific methods (laboratory analysis or statistics) and the
degree of precision required to support the claim about tobacco
and cancer.

During most of the Twentieth Century a cigarette was the sign
of cool for many different people, and one brand was aptly labeled
"Cool" for a mentholated cigarette. For adolescents, a smoke was a
sign of adulthood, and for women it signaled liberation; for the lonely,
the question "Would you care for a smoke?" was the beginning of a
conversation and perhaps a relationship. Smoking was normalized
almost everywhere. It was permitted on airplanes, in hospital waiting
rooms and doctors' offices,[13] in restaurants, in college classrooms, and

---

[13] At a time when the doctor stood out in the public mind as the quintessential "man"
of science, Camel's slogan was "More doctors smoke Camels than any other brand,"

in films – *especially* in films. During the Second World War, Camel shipped free cigarettes to servicemen fighting in Europe and Asia, and after the war, Winston representatives would hand out free samples at many colleges, including Boston University, my alma mater, a then nominally Methodist institution, whose administration claimed to frown on smoking and drinking. But still many of my professors, including the dean of the Liberal Arts College, my honors advisor, chain-smoked along with many of the students.

The culture favored smokers over nonsmokers, and it would often take considerable courage to ask a smoker if he or she – by that time many women smoked – would mind not smoking. Usually the nonsmoker would feel obliged to give some kind of excuse for the request – my asthma is acting up, or I have a really bad cold. Even then there might often be grandiose sighs, a rolling of the eyes, signs of affected affirmations, indicating both displeasure with the request and as a signal that the request actually trespassed on the rights of the smoker.

The change that occurred is a powerful example of the way in which basic democratic principles along with technical scientific research can combine to produce powerful cultural changes. Even when the research demonstrated the connection between smoking and cancer, many were still reluctant to quit smoking. The fact that it was a powerful addictive agent, consciously and cynically formulated by companies to increase addiction, made it even harder to do so. Putting aside the overt lies by the heads of tobacco companies,[14] one

and Lucky Strike insisted that "20,679 physicians say Luckies are less irritating." And the truth was that many of these men – and they were men – of science were indeed smokers. The complicity of the medical profession – Camel would reportedly give doctors a carton of Camels before asking them what they smoked – was not because there was something wrong with the organic chemistry or pharmacology that medical students were required to take. It was simply the fact that those subjects were not the ones needed to understand this particular pandemic. See Allan M. Brandt, *The Cigarette Century: The Rise, Fall, and Deadly Persistence of the Product that Defined America* (New York: Basic Books, 2007).

[14] "The Five Ways Heads of Tobacco Companies Lied about the Dangers of Smoking" (online); available at https://truthinitiative.org/research-resources/tobacco-prevention-efforts/5-ways-tobacco-companies-lied-about-dangers-smoking.

of the things that made a big difference was research on the harm that secondhand smoke did to nonsmokers, initiating a change from "Yes, you have a right to choose to kill yourself" to "But you do not have a right to kill me!" Over a relatively short period of time, smoking became less cool, and smokers were eventually granted minor pariah status.

DEMOCRACY AS A DECIDING FACTOR: A CLASH OF VALUES

The research that found that secondhand smoke was harmful to innocent nonsmokers negated the relevance of the anti-paternalism principle, while still drawing on the democratic consensus. For while democracy and the idea of individual freedom limits the right of one person or the state to compel another to do what is in her own best interest, it sets a limit on the freedom of one person to impinge on the freedom of another. Hence, while I cannot tell you to do what is in your own best interest, I can require you not to harm me. So, if you want to smoke, by all means do so, but not in my restaurant, or my home, or on the seat next to me on the bus, train, or plane.

As a smoker at the time, I literally experienced the cultural ground shift. One year I gave a paper at a conference at Oxford University and had a terrible cold. The room was filled with smoke, and it was only after considerable coughing and hesitation that I asked if members of the audience would stop smoking. Most did, but many looked visibly annoyed. A couple of years later, I went to another conference, also at Oxford, and noticed that many smokers felt obliged to ask, "Do you mind if I smoke?" That year most people did grant permission, but a few years later, most did not. After a while people stopped asking, and smokers just went outside to light up, and then, after a few more years, many, myself included, had stopped smoking.

By shifting the burden of proof from nonsmoker to smoker, the receptiveness of a public to scientific research had enabled a major cultural change to take place, and this cultural shift precipitated changes in policy and law. Privately owned airlines and restaurants first restricted smoking to certain sections, and then they banned smoking altogether, just as states began to consider legislation that prohibited smoking in any confined public space. In the end, the actual change was rather simple. Smoking was never banned completely. It was just made increasingly difficult to smoke, as the public mood changed from acceptance to reluctance and then to anger or pity for those who still insist on lighting up. Or, to put it differently, science precipitated a reconstruction of an implicit public syllogism in which the anti-paternalism principle was the major premise. The anti-paternalism principle was never really rejected, but it was no longer seen to be relevant as a guide to the relationship between smoker and nonsmoker. It was then replaced by the self-preservation principle that allows you to limit the harm that my smoking does to you.

While the logic of this change is largely implicit, no official emerged to declare: "Henceforth the anti-paternalism principle does not apply to the relation between smoker and nonsmokers. From now on the 'you may not harm me' principle applies." As it now stands, most nonsmokers can comfortably ask any smoker to put out her cigarette or leave the room, assuming that smoking is even allowed.

A reconstruction of the logic that eventually was accepted by the public fails to adequately capture the details of the decades of debates that finally allowed the right question, "Is smoking safe?" to emerge over the much less urgent one, "Exactly what might the ingredient in tobacco be that leads to cancer?" Granted, the process by which citizens came to accept the fact that tobacco played a significant role in cancer-related deaths was long and messy, and my reconstructing of the everyday logic cannot do justice to the obfuscation and distractions used by the tobacco industry to confuse the public. But one of the educational aims of a rational reconstruction is to enable rising citizens to recognize similar situations – say climate change – and to use knowledge of the behavior of bad actors in the past to recognize the misuse of science in the present.

CONCLUSION: IMPORTANCE OF CORRECT CALIBRATION

One important science lesson of the debate over cigarettes and cancer is that the methods and the standards of exactitude that scientists employ can change, and the change can influence the conclusions they draw. Given the rigor of math and science, many students will assume that the more rigorous the method, and the higher the standard of exactitude, the better the science. Yet the soundness of this assumption depends on the nature of the subject matter and the purpose of the task. For example, if Dr. Kelsey had waited until the exact causal mechanism was known, many more babies would have been born with deformed limbs. On the other hand, the later discovery of a causal mechanism allowed additional progress to be made on safe ways to use the drug as a treatment for other conditions.

A goal of science education for the custodians of democracy then should be to provide a more refined understanding of the appropriateness of different methods for different situations. The aim here is to help students understand that the scientific method is neither rigid nor uniform; the choice of a method involves a choice about the desired standard of precision, which is context dependent. In some situations (e.g., the *Challenger* disaster), an insistence on precision is critical, but in others (e.g., cigarettes) a premature insistence on too much precision can actually enhance risk. The task for the custodian of democracy, whether serving as producers or consumers of scientific innovation, is to bring the relationship between science and human values back into focus, and to develop in students the habit of asking just what is at stake and what level of precision is appropriate for different scientific endeavors and different human concerns.

8   The Expressive Curriculum

INTRODUCTION

In 2001, a few days after 9/11, following the World Trade Center bombing in New York City, a bagpipe band, blasting Sousa marches, stormed out of a bar on State Street in Chicago as I was passing by. I felt a strong physical compulsion to keep in step with the music but hesitated because the band seemed to buttress the sporadic anti-Muslim violence that was reported to be occurring throughout the country. In that context, the Sousa march had a menacing quality, and I tried, with difficulty, to walk out of step to the beat.

Now walking out of step to the music has never been difficult for me – I can do it on a dance floor easily – but this time I felt trapped by the martial beat of the music. To avoid being controlled by the rhythm of the band, I had to actually stop walking until the music faded into the distance. Only then was I able to amble at my own unregimented pace.

I recall this incident to illustrate the power of music and other art forms to control emotions and motivate action. Music and art in general seem to touch our emotions directly, affecting both mood and behavior. Indeed, the source of the word *emotion* is from the Latin *emovere*, meaning to move, to agitate, to excite, and to stir. The struggle between my willing legs and my reluctant head represents a larger tension within citizenship education, one between the need for social cohesion and the need for distance and critical reflection.

THE TENSION BETWEEN THE NEED FOR SOCIAL COHESION AND THE NEED FOR CRITICAL REFLECTION

This chapter addresses the role of the "expressive curriculum," a term I use that includes the educative role of public monuments, as well as art and music, in advancing the twin needs of democracy for both social cohesion and critical reflection. Social cohesion involves the moral integration of society and refers to the degree to which members of society can depend on one another to exercise critical social virtues, such as honesty, mutual trust, restraint, and a willingness to sacrifice individual interest to address a collective imperative. Critical reflection is the capacity to step outside of one's daily habits and commitments to assess a situation in its larger context. Without critical reflection, social cohesion becomes autocratic and tyrannical. Without social cohesion, critical reflection becomes self-centered and anarchical. But these two are not always easily reconciled, as Plato understood when he advocated the "Noble Lie" in order to promote social cohesion; nor is it easily reconcilable for those who view social cohesion as simply the seeds of irrational, uncritical authoritarianism.

THE EXPRESSIVE CURRICULUM AND BUILDING A SENSE OF BELONGING

Democracy promotes personal initiative and individual flourishing. It encourages people to act on their own behalf, to decide for themselves how to live their own lives, and to pursue their own conception of good. And yet society also needs at times to call on these same individuals to put aside their own concerns, to view themselves as a part of a larger body, and to exercise certain collective virtues.[1] As Dewey noted, the very idea of a society depends on each individual developing a sense of partnership in a shared activity, a sense that depends on the development of shared ideas and emotions.[2] Without this sense, all that we have is an aggregate of individuals, each acting for his or her self-perceived best interest.

---

[1] Eric Bredo, "Culture Wars, Durkheim and Moral Education," paper presented at the American Educational Studies Association Meeting, Pittsburgh, PA, November 4–8, 1992. Personal correspondence.

[2] John Dewey, *Democracy and Education: An Introduction to the Philosophy of Education* (New York: The Free Press, 1916/1944), p. 13.

As Randy Martin observes, art plays a significant role in informing us about the nature of these collective virtues and in aiding their development.

> Art can be considered a particular kind of social good that serves as a means to bring forth ideas about our lives together. In this, public art performs a civic function. It seeks to make explicit linkages among the formal properties of a work, its ability to get us to pay attention to our surroundings, and how we value what we perceive. In this, the form and content of public art is fundamentally about how we live together with those around us. Such work rests on a conviction that art is not simply aesthetically enlivening of everyday surroundings but that it is civically ennobling. The representational aspect runs a thread through the history of public art. The monuments of old, "the hero on the horse," exalted great historical figures around which a nation might be unified that characterized the explosion of nineteenth-century civic sculpture. The populist turn, epitomized by the murals of Diego Rivera in the 1930's rendered everyday life and ordinary people worthy of artistic memorialization. Community-based works like those of John Ahearn in the mid-1980's and early '90s explored a yet more intimate relation between the artist and certain residents he selected to be models for his sculptures. In each of these examples, art is treated as the embodiment of shared values – of the nation, public, or community – and serves to integrate through its own legible forms those who might otherwise remain strangers to one another.[3]

The expressive curriculum is central in building a sense of belonging and stamping the identity of rising citizens, and also in shifting our attention to emerging critical issues. Think, for example, of the quilt

---

[3] Randy Martin, "Artistic Citizenship: Introduction," in Mary Schmidt Campbell and Randy Martin, eds., *Artistic Citizenship: A Public Voice for the Arts* (New York: Routledge, 2006), p. 3.

memorial in honor of the people who died of AIDS. Yet the expressive curriculum is also a major cite of contestation and struggle.

DEMOCRACY AND CULTURAL BELONGING

Democracy has two sides, a political one and a cultural one. The first is about governance; the second is about belonging and growth. Political democracy usually traces its philosophical origins back to John Locke who stressed the idea that democracy is rooted in the authority of individual citizens, and its main goal is to maintain order and settle disputes. Cultural democracy can be traced to the philosopher Johann Gottfried Herder (1744–1803), among others, and the idea that human potential could only be realized by belonging to a congenial, nurturing group. Although Herder identified the nation as such a group, today many see cultural attachment as playing the same role. For Herder, each (national) group had its own specific character that he thought was reflected in its unique art, music, and moral code.[4]

The two sides of democracy, the political and the cultural, are tied together by their recognition of the importance of individual expression. Political democracy emphasizes the expression of individual opinion; cultural democracy emphasizes the socially imbedded, individual self – its uniqueness and potential – what some today call the "authentic self." Herder believed that individual potential could only be developed by and through membership in a caring and convivial group.[5] The view that there is an authentic Black art or an authentic Mexican art, for example, is a modern-day echo of Herder's idea. The scornful claim that the *established* literary and artistic canon is an imposition[6] on minority cultures is the other side of the same view. The scorn is an expression of two related moods.

[4] Granted Herder's emphasis on national character complicates his relation to democracy.
[5] While Herder held that the nation was that group, today his description better fits our idea of primary cultural groups existing inside of a multicultural country.
[6] Pierre Bourdieu and Jean-Claude Passeron, *Reproduction in Education, Society and Culture* (London: Sage, 1977).

The first is a rejection of the right of a dominant cultural form to be imposed on a cultural minority. The second is a protest against a majority co-opting the cultural form of a minority. Consider Ralph Gleason's protest against white people appropriating the Blues.

> The blues is black man's [sic] music, and whites diminish it at best or steal it at worst. In any case they have no moral right to use it.[7]

When Gleason rejects the idea that white people can play the blues,[8] likely because they don't have the needed background cultural experience, he echoes Herder's view that art is and must be a unique cultural expression. He also implicitly rejects the popular idea that art is universal.

This raises important questions not only about Herder but also about the nature of social cohesion. At one extreme, Herder's ethnic nationalism has been incorrectly connected with the founding of National Socialism and the Nazi party. At the other it is connected to modern anthropology and the view that all cultural expressions have a unique quality deserving of respect but also that full understanding across cultural divides is unattainable.[9] For the education of custodians of democracy, it raises the question of what kind of social cohesion is desirable in a multicultural, liberal democracy.

THE ROLE OF THE EXPRESSIVE CURRICULUM
IN THE CULTIVATION OF POLITICAL FRIENDSHIP

Social cohesion involves a sense of membership and participation in a common enterprise. Cohesion entails an enterprise where every

---

[7] Ralph Gleason quoted in Joel Rudinow, "Race, Ethnicity, Expressive Authenticity: Can White People Sing the Blues?" *Journal of Aesthetics and Art Criticism*, 52(1) (Winter 1994), 127–137.

[8] For an insightful analysis of this claim, see Imran Rahman-Jones, "White People, Blues Music and the Problem of Cultural Appropriation"; available at medium.com/RahmanJones/white-people-music-and-the-problem-of cultural-appropriation-3eb61b8d25c03.

[9] For my extended response to the question of understanding across cultures, see my *Common Schools/Uncommon Identities*.

person sees themselves as benefiting from the efforts of all – including those of past participants – and where each person identifies with and attempts to contribute, to the best of their ability, to the well-being of all, including future participants. Democratic cohesion requires a sense of empathy across differences where everyone, regardless of birth, ultimately holds equal rank as citizen and, as citizen, is entitled to equal voice, fair treatment, and similar respect. Developing a sense of empathy is part of the work of the expressive curriculum. It is developed by many art forms. Take, for example, Shylock's plea in Shakespeare's *The Merchant of Venice*:

> I am a Jew. Hath not a Jew eyes? Hath not a Jew hands, organs, dimensions, senses, affections, passions: fed with the same food, hurt with the same weapons, subject to the same disease.[10]

Suffering, whether it be of the Jew in *The Merchant of Venice* or of the lynched Black people in Billie Holiday's song *Strange Fruit*, becomes an object for artistic expression when the artist draws on a particular experience to activate an emotional connection that has universal connotations. Rising citizens can be easily shortchanged by well-intended people wishing to censor works out of understandable fears about the way one group or another is portrayed, or because, like Gleason, they want to assert cultural authenticity as a kind of property right.

Danielle Allen, following Aristotle, describes the extension of sentiments from the first-person perspective to the perspective of the generalized other as "political friendship" or the kind of relationship strangers have when they "feel … that their relationship rests on equality: each must believe that the relationship's benefits and burdens are shared more or less equally; each friend needs equal recognition from the other; and each needs an equal agency within the relationship."[11] Democratic cohesion, best conceived of as

---

[10] William Shakespeare, *The Merchant of Venice* (New Haven: Yale University Press, 1957, 3.1) p. 46.
[11] Danielle S. Allen, *Talking to Strangers: Anxieties of Citizenship since* Brown v. Board of Education (Chicago: University of Chicago Press, 2004), p. 129.

movement from the experience of particular people to a concern that can touch all, is not self-sustaining; it requires care and attention.

POLITICAL FRIENDSHIP AS AN AIM
OF THE EXPRESSIVE CURRICULUM

The development of political friendship among strangers is one of the aims of the expressive curriculum, as it is represented in public monuments, as well as canonical art. Political friendship is formed through shared, common experience. For an experience to be shared, people must undergo it either directly, say, as an immigrant or a soldier in battle, or indirectly through literature, music, or public art, such as the Statue of Liberty or the Vietnam Memorial. For an experience to be common, everyone must have a reasonable expectation that it is shared in a similar way by others, and there must be opportunities to make this expectation visible to all. This is accomplished through art or civic enactments.

SHAPING AND MODIFYING THE EXPRESSIVE CURRICULUM

As custodians of democracy, there is a need to be aware of the constructed nature of the expressive curriculum and to address harmful misrepresentations, sometimes by marching out of step to the music, sometimes with a more public act of resistance. This requires the recognition, as Leo Tolstoy argued, that art exists for more than art's sake.

> Art ... is a human activity consisting in this, that one man
> consciously, by means of certain external signs, hands on to others
> feelings he has lived through, and that other people are infected by
> these feelings and also experience them.[12]

Art, as Tolstoy puts it, is "one of the means of intercourse between man and man."[13] According to Tolstoy, we do not have to consult

---

[12] Leo N. Tolstoy, *What Is Art?* (Indianapolis: Hackett Publishing Company, 1896/ 1996), p. 51.
[13] Ibid., p. 49.

great art in order to appreciate the impact that artistic representation can have on human relationships. "All human life is filled with works of art of every kind – from cradlesong, jest, mimicry, the ornamentation of houses ... So that by art, in the limited sense of the word, we do not mean all human activity transmitting feelings, but only that part which we for some reason select from it and to which we attach special importance."[14]

Just how a group is represented and who is promoted to represent it are critical considerations for selecting works that are to be presented as canonical. As the philosopher Charles Taylor observes,

> A person or group of people can suffer real damage, real distortion if the people or society around them mirror back to them a confining or demeaning or contemptible picture of themselves.
>
> Nonrecognition or misrecognition can inflict harm, can be a form of oppression, imprisoning someone in a false, distorted, and reduced model of being.[15]

Recognition and misrecognition can be determined by many things, large and seemingly small. For example, it makes a difference where a statue of Robert E. Lee is located. Put it in the city center and it says, here is a hero: venerate him! Clearly, this is a slight to the African American experience of slavery, which Lee fought to defend. Place the statue in a history museum, and it could be read in many different ways, perhaps as a tragic figure, perhaps as a historical villain, perhaps as a symbol of a lost cause or of a vain, inhuman period. Democracy does not dictate feeling.

THE EVOLVING EXPRESSIVE CURRICULUM

The Expressive Curriculum changes as people confront new conditions and develop new ways to understand past events. Consider, for

---

[14] Ibid., pp. 52–53.
[15] Charles Taylor, *Multiculturalism and the Politics of Recognition* (Princeton: Princeton University Press, 1992), p. 25.

example, the changes in poetry about the American Revolution in response to major issues of different times.

> Many of the most important and memorable poems that have been written about the American Revolution are really not about the revolution at all; or, to put it more precisely, they were not written with the American Revolution primarily in view. "Paul Revere's Ride," for example, is a vigorous patriotic ballad; it did much to stimulate the martial spirit of northerners; and, appearing as it did at the beginning of the Civil War, the message of the final stanza was perfectly plain:
>
>> For, borne on the night-wind of the past,
>> Through all our history, to the last,
>> In the hour of darkness and peril and need,
>> The people will waken and listen to hear
>> The hurrying hoof-beats of that steed
>> And the midnight message of Paul Revere.[16]

Here Henry Wadsworth Longfellow's poem glosses a past moment to express a desired future outcome.

AN EXAMPLE OF PRODUCTIVE CHANGE

Many years ago, when my wife and I visited Thomas Jefferson's estate at Monticello, the guide, a white woman, never mentioned Jefferson's slaves or his relationship with Sally Hemings, his slave mistress. When I asked about the topic of slavery, the guide adroitly avoided the topic.

According to Clint Smith's excellent book on the legacy of slavery and Jim Crow, *How the Word Is Passed*,[17] this has changed, and Monticello tours now incorporate the story of Jefferson's enslaved

---

[16] Michael Kammen, *A Season of Youth: The American Revolution and Historical Imagination* (Ithaca: Cornell University Press, 1978), p. 122.

[17] Clint Smith, *How the Word Is Passed: A Reckoning with the History of Slavery across America* (New York: Little, Brown, 2021), pp. 39–47.

people. They also no longer hide his relationship with Hemings. As David, a thirty-year retired military officer and now a tour guide at Monticello, commented during Smith's more recent visit:

> There is a chapter on the *Notes of Virginia* ... that has some of the most racist things you might ever read ... So sometimes I stop and ask myself "If Gettysburg had gone the wrong way, would people be quoting the Declaration of Independence or *Notes on the State of Virginia*?" It's the same guy writing both.[18]

David continues:

> So, I believe in the idea of America. I don't believe that this country *was* perfect. I don't believe it's going to *be* perfect. I believe that the journey to make this a better place is worth the effort and that the United States, if you conceive it not so much a place to be in but an idea to believe in, it is worth fighting for.[19]

The expressive curriculum can be a powerful weapon in this fight, encouraging the rising citizens to glimpse a more inclusive possible future. The educational challenge is to be able to do this while not imposing a preferred meaning on iconic representations and while allowing critical thinking to flourish. Consider the following example.

THE EMANCIPATION STATUE

A bronze memorial – the Emancipation – has stood in Lincoln Park in Washington, DC, since 1876, with a replica in Boston. It was sculpted to commemorate Lincoln's Emancipation Proclamation that symbolically ended legalized slavery in the Confederate states. The funds for the statue were provided through the efforts of Charlotte Scott and other freed slaves – to my mind a remarkable effort. Frederick Douglass gave the keynote address at the unveiling. The work depicts President Lincoln standing over and looking down on a partially clothed Black man, the formerly enslaved Archer Alexander, who is

[18] Ibid., p. 40.   [19] Ibid., p. 42.

looking up at Lincoln. Douglass's address captures in essence the sentiments expressed by both sides, today:

> It must be admitted, truth compels me to admit, even here in the
> presence of the monument we have erected to his memory,
> Abraham Lincoln was not, in the fullest sense of the word,
> either our man or our model. In his interests, in his associations,
> in his habits of thought, and in his prejudices, he was a
> white man.
>
> He was preeminently the white man's President, entirely devoted
> to the welfare of white men. He was ready and willing at any time
> during the first years of his administration to deny, postpone, and
> sacrifice the rights of humanity in the colored people to promote
> the welfare of the white people of this country. In all his education
> and feeling he was an American of the Americans. He came into the
> Presidential chair upon one principle alone, namely, opposition to
> the extension of slavery. His arguments in furtherance of this policy
> had their motive and mainspring in his patriotic devotion to the
> interests of his own race. To protect, defend, and perpetuate slavery
> in the states where it existed Abraham Lincoln was not less ready
> than any other President to draw the sword of the nation. He was
> ready to execute all the supposed guarantees of the United States
> Constitution in favor of the slave system anywhere inside the slave
> states. He was willing to pursue, recapture, and send back the
> fugitive slave to his master, and to suppress a slave rising for liberty,
> though his guilty master were already in arms against the
> Government. The race to which we belong were not the special
> objects of his consideration. Knowing this, I concede to you, my
> white fellow-citizens, a preeminence in this worship at once full
> and supreme. First, midst, and last, you and yours were the objects
> of his deepest affection and his most earnest solicitude. You are the
> children of Abraham Lincoln. We are at best only his stepchildren;
> children by adoption, children by forces of circumstances and
> necessity. To you it especially belongs to sound his praises, to

preserve and perpetuate his memory, to multiply his statues, to hang his pictures high upon your walls, and commend his example, for to you he was a great and glorious friend and benefactor. Instead of supplanting you at his altar, we would exhort you to build high his monuments; let them be of the most costly material, of the most cunning workmanship; let their forms be symmetrical, beautiful, and perfect; let their bases be upon solid rocks, and their summits lean against the unchanging blue, overhanging sky, and let them endure forever! But while in the abundance of your wealth, and in the fullness of your just and patriotic devotion, you do all this, we entreat you to despise not the humble offering we this day unveil to view; for while Abraham Lincoln saved for you a country, he delivered us from a bondage, according to Jefferson, one hour of which was worse than ages of the oppression your fathers rose in rebellion to oppose.

I have said that President Lincoln was a white man, and shared the prejudices common to his countrymen towards the colored race. Looking back to his times and to the condition of his country, we are compelled to admit that this unfriendly feeling on his part may be safely set down as one element of his wonderful success in organizing the loyal American people for the tremendous conflict before them, and bringing them safely through that conflict. His great mission was to accomplish two things: first, to save his country from dismemberment and ruin; and, second, to free his country from the great crime of slavery. To do one or the other, or both, he must have the earnest sympathy and the powerful cooperation of his loyal fellow-countrymen. Without this primary and essential condition to success his efforts must have been vain and utterly fruitless. Had he put the abolition of slavery before the salvation of the Union, he would have inevitably driven from him a powerful class of the American people and rendered resistance to rebellion impossible. Viewed from the genuine abolition ground, Mr. Lincoln seemed tardy, cold, dull, and indifferent; but measuring him by the sentiment of his country, a sentiment he was bound as a statesman to consult, he was swift, zealous, radical, and determined.[20]

As mentioned, recently considerable controversy has come to public attention over the significance of the statue, and some Black people now demand it be removed. The advocates for its removal point out that the Black person is represented in a subservient position, and they note the work failed to acknowledge the role that Black people themselves played in their own emancipation, a role that has become clearer in recent years as scholars, especially Black scholars, have been informing us of the role that enslaved and formerly enslaved people played in shaping their own emancipation and education,[21] as well as their resistance to enslavement.

In part the debate depends on just how you see the Black figure. Is he kneeling? In which case the statue reinforces the idea of Black people as subservient. Or is he rising? In which case he represents a coming to be free. Or, to take a different view, he could be becoming, reaching toward the day when the statue itself becomes an object of controversy as it becomes clearer that freedom is never just given, but is the result of a struggle and co-constructed. The debate calls for an interpretation, including a fuller understanding of how the statue was received at the time. And it is in the initiation of critical thinking that the present debate has its most educational significance, and makes it a work worthy of educational attention. Douglass got it just right when he spoke the last words of his inaugural address:

> Though Mr. Lincoln shared the prejudices of his white fellow-countrymen against the Negro, it is hardly necessary to say that in

---

[20] Frederick Douglass, "Oration in Memory of Abraham Lincoln," delivered at the unveiling of the Freedmen's Monument in memory of Abraham Lincoln, in Lincoln Park, Washington, DC, April 14, 1876 (online); available at https://rbscp.lib .rochester.edu/4402.

[21] James D. Anderson, *The Education of Blacks in the South, 1860–1935* (Chapel Hill: University of North Carolina Press, 1988) provides a comprehensive examination of the work of formerly enslaved people and other Blacks to shape their own educational experience.

his heart of hearts he loathed and hated slavery. ... The man who could say, "Fondly do we hope, fervently do we pray, that this mighty scourge of war shall soon pass away, yet if God wills it continue till all the wealth piled by two hundred years of bondage shall have been wasted, and each drop of blood drawn by the lash shall have been paid for by one drawn by the sword, the judgments of the Lord are true and righteous altogether," gives all needed proof of his feeling on the subject of slavery. He was willing, while the South was loyal, that it should have its pound of flesh, because he thought that it was so nominated in the bond; but farther than this no earthly power could make him go.[22]

THE INTERPRETIVE TURN: CALIBRATING THE CANON TOWARD EQUALITY

In capturing the complexities of Lincoln, Douglass speaks to a very contemporary issue – how are we to understand the contributions of flawed canonical figures, who are mostly white and mostly men? And then, exactly what makes them flawed? That is, what standard of judgment is appropriate for evaluating iconic representation? A closer look at Douglass's speech can begin to provide answers.

Consider, for example, the passage "His [Lincoln's] arguments in furtherance of this policy had their motive and mainspring in his patriotic devotion to the interests of his own race." Here Douglass understands that the monument will have different meanings for white and for Black people, and he addresses white people as a "you" through the eyes of we, Black people. When he appeals to white people as "my white fellow-citizens," he glosses Lincoln's Gettysburg Address and the "new birth of freedom" that it promised. However, as

---

[22] Frederick Douglass, "Oration in Memory of Abraham Lincoln," delivered at the unveiling of the Freedmen's Monument in memory of Abraham Lincoln, in Lincoln Park, Washington, DC, April 14, 1876 (online); available at https://rbscp.lib .rochester.edu/4402.

he does so, he acknowledges the very different standings that whites and Blacks have in this birth – one the child, the other the stepchild.

> Knowing this, I concede to you, my white fellow-citizens, a preeminence in this worship at once full and supreme. First, midst, and last, you and yours were the objects of his deepest affection and his most earnest solicitude. You are the children of Abraham Lincoln. We are at best only his stepchildren; children by adoption, children by forces of circumstances and necessity.[23]

The observation might have been an occasion for fanning flames of resentment: "Viewed from the genuine abolition ground, Mr. Lincoln seemed tardy, cold, dull, and indifferent."

But Douglass refuses to go there:

> [B]ut measuring him by the sentiment of his country, a sentiment he was bound as a statesman to consult, he was swift, zealous, radical, and determined. Had he put the abolition of slavery before the salvation of the Union, he would have inevitably driven from him a powerful class of the American people and rendered resistance to rebellion impossible.[24]

Douglass does not tell future generations where to focus their gaze or how to understand the statue. Rather he understands the dedication as a moment in a larger, yet to be completed, struggle, one where the meaning of canonical displays can evolve. He does not tell future generations the "right" way to see it. As with the function of any true artwork, he leaves its meaning to be negotiated between artist and viewer and allows for changing time and social context to modify meaning.

The recent protests over the statue can illustrate this evolutionary advance. Douglass's focus was completely on Lincoln and the

---

[23] Ibid.

[24] Frederick Douglass, "Oration in Memory of Abraham Lincoln," delivered at the unveiling of the Freedmen's Monument in memory of Abraham Lincoln, in Lincoln Park, Washington, DC, April 14, 1876 (online); available at https://rbscp.lib .rochester.edu/4402.

meaning that should be attributed to him. He said nothing about the figure of the Black man, Archer Alexander, crouched at Lincoln's side. Alexander had been enslaved before the Civil War. Today, however, the focus has partly shifted from Lincoln to Alexander, from the "liberator" to the "liberated." In this shift, the role of formerly enslaved persons in their own emancipation is acknowledged. Without this recognition, emancipation remains a gift rather than an outcome of a struggle that continues. The debate itself signals that emancipation is not over, but that it is a continuing process, and that democratic cohesion will always be a work in progress, a work that is both shaped by and shapes the expressive curriculum.

CAN WHITE PEOPLE PLAY THE BLUES?

Return to Herder's idea that each nation (or in contemporary terms, each culture) has its own aesthetics, its own sense of beauty that only it can express. Of course, to any Black artist who has ever played a Mozart concerto, this claim would appear ridiculous, and yet there is something to it that needs to be considered. Perhaps because of the unique brutality of slavery and Jim Crow and the very specific quality that it took to survive with dignity in a country that viewed itself as that wonderful "City on a Hill" – the new Jerusalem – there is something to the view that the blues express a very different kind of collective experience. As Rudinow explains:

> The authenticity of a blues performance turns not on the ethnicity of the performer but on the degree of the mastery of the idiom and the integrity of the performer's use of the idiom in performance.[25]

The correct conclusion is not that white people cannot play the blues, but rather that without an initiation into the cultural experience out of which the blues developed, the playing will likely be superficial, a sequence of sounds – not an expression of a powerful cultural

---

[25] Rudinow, "Race, Ethnicity, Expressive Authenticity," p. 135.

experience. Ultimately, however, authenticity depends on the possibility of cultural evolution and growth.[26]

But Herder had a similar concern – "how can the individual or the nation remain firmly grounded in its own native foundation ... and at the same time so extend its horizons as to absorb the thoughts and works of other individuals in other cultures without which there can be no possibility of a full human existence?"[27]

Art purism is a misconception and hides the universal elements in art and music. European cubism was inspired by African masks, which were exhibited in Paris in the early 1900s.[28] African tradition as well as European harmonics and field calls among enslaved people are claimed to be influences on the formation of the early blues.[29] And then in turn, the blues are said to have influenced country music as well as rock.

While art and music play critical roles in shaping cultural and national identities, aesthetic forms rarely are sui generis. As Fouss-Feinberg shows in his analysis of East Timor music, independence movements use music to forge a national identity, and in doing so may borrow on many different musical traditions, including those of the colonizer, to create a new and unique sound.[30]

RESHAPING THE EXPRESSIVE CURRICULUM

The expressive curriculum is not just a given. It is also a taken. It is made and remade by human actors hoping to shape the meaning of the past for the sake of a particular kind of future. For custodians of

---

[26] Ibid.

[27] Michael Morton, "Herder: The Poetics of Thought: Unity and Diversity," in *On Diligence in Several Learned Languages* (University Park: Penn State University Press, 1988), p. 18.

[28] Arvind Rajagopal, "Art for Art Sake? Artistic Citizenship as an Uncertain Thing," in Mary Schmidt Campbell and Randy Martin, eds., *Artistic Citizenship: A Public Voice for the Arts* (New York: Routledge, 2006), p. 137.

[29] History of the Blues (online); available at https://awblues.weebly.com/african-influences-on-the-blues.html.

[30] Austin Fouss-Feinberg, "Yampolsky Files: An Analysis," unpublished class paper for University of Illinois MUS 418, December 19, 2018.

democracy, this future will be guided by a sense of openness and inclusiveness. But as new visions are added, the meaning of older, more established ones will need to be renewed and refitted – the term "woke" is the most recent expression of the culmination of this process. If the expressive curriculum is to evolve toward openness and inclusiveness, the past must be recognized by the present. Consider the song "America the Beautiful" to see how the present can give new and added meaning to the past.

"America the Beautiful" is a lovely song, more harmonious and more poetic than the "Star Spangled Banner." Nevertheless, it does have a history that needs to be addressed. The words "And crown thy good with brotherhood *from sea to shining sea*" were first published in 1904, revising the original lyrics from 1895. They were sung in a celebratory tone just as the country's "Manifest Destiny" had been realized "from sea to shining sea."[31]

The song, as originally sung, represented the spirit of the times, echoing in music the flawed observation by historian Frederick Jackson Turner that the period of the frontier as an *empty wilderness* had come to an end.[32] "America the Beautiful" imagined an American wilderness empty of civilized communities – the blank page upon which this new map could be drawn. That void remains part of the musical canon. Native Americans were not part of the imagined map, nor could they be a part of the shared vision that was America in the making. Today, placing the song in its larger historical context, one that brings back into view the cost of that expansion to Native Americans, sanctions an alternative performance – mournful as well as celebratory and played in a minor as well as a major key.[33]

[31] And beyond as Puerto Rico, Guam, and Hawaii were added in 1898. See Daniel Immerwahr, *How to Hide an Empire: A History of the Greater United States* (New York: Farrar, Straus and Giroux, 2019).

[32] Frederick Jackson Turner, "The Frontier in American History" (University of Arizona Press, 1986).

[33] Appreciation to Fouss-Feinberg for this observation.

It also suggests a new vision of cultural identity, one best expressed by Stuart Hall:

> Cultural identity ... is a matter of "becoming" as well as of "being." It belongs to the future as much as to the past.... Cultural identities come from somewhere, have histories. But like everything which is historical, they undergo constant transformation. Far from being eternally fixed in some essentialized past, they are subject to the continuous "play" of history, culture and power.... Identities are the names we give to the different ways we are positioned by, and position ourselves within, the narratives of the past.[34]

Society encompasses the patterns of interaction of these semi-independent points of similarity and difference; democratic social cohesion is determined by the quality of that interaction and by how well it facilitates informed participation and growth both within and between groups.

CONCLUSION: WHY DOES IT MATTER?

Some might argue that inclusion or exclusion from something as amorphous and open ended as *the* expressive curriculum, or, what some call "the canon" is of little consequence. Indeed, it might be argued that the very idea of *a* canon is misleading. Different groups have their own music and art, and in a free society, this is the way it should be. But surely it makes a difference when the historical experience of a group is distorted, or when the suffering of one group is ignored in order to promote the purported heroism of another – think of the monuments to Southern generals. But the significance is wider than the impact on the group whose experience is distorted or ignored. As Parysa Clare Mostajir, following Dewey, argues:

> Sustaining a democratic society ... requires the communication of experiences between diverse groups, not only to create

---

[34] Stuart Hall, "Cultural Identity and Diaspora," in Jonathan Rutherford, ed., *Identity: Community, Culture, Difference* (London: Lawrence & Wishart, 1990), p. 225.

representative shared interpretations of social reality, but to
democratize the conceptual resources with which we
collectively reproduce or readjust our institutional policies and
material arrangements. The ability to control the circulation of
narratives and impose partial perspectives on a society's share
interpretive resources is "a crucial dimension of any power
regime" ..., while in contrast, a "society which makes provisions
for participation in its good of all its members on equal terms and
which secures flexible readjustment of its institutions through
interactions of different forms of associative life is in so far
democratic."[35]

The capacity of artistic works to speak directly to the emotions – to
move us in one way or another – is a critical consideration in determining how an experience is to be represented and who should do the
representation. When significant groups are left out of the national
story, or when some groups dominate the storytelling, distortion is a
likely result. But the distortion is not only of the past experience; it
continues to influence the present and the future. It is what Fricker
insightfully labels "hermeneutical injustice" (i.e., "having some significant area of one's social experience obscured from collective
understanding").[36] It perpetuates harm. A powerful response to this
harm comes from those who have been left out or whose experience
has been distorted. Protest art in the form of a quilt memorializing
those who have died of AIDS and community theater bringing
members of a group in dialogue with one another, and with those
from different traditions, are ways to begin to penetrate and challenge
these distortions.

Finally, and again, the authors of the Constitution were quite
prescient when they chose the phrase "a more perfect union," perhaps

[35] Parysa Clare Mostajir, "Conjoint Communicative Experience: Art as an Instrument
of Democracy," *The Pluralist: The Journal of the Society for the Advancement of
American Philosophy*, 17(1) (Spring 2022), 27.
[36] Quoted in ibid., p. 29.

recognizing the limitations that one's own times places on the capacity of oppressed individuals – think of gay or transgender people – to come together as a coherent group to demand proper recognition and for the larger society to begin to grasp just what this might mean for the extension of justice and domestic tranquility.

9 Democratic Education and Moral Growth

[Society] is a partnership in all science, a partnership in all art, a partnership in every virtue and in all perfection. As the ends of such a partnership cannot be obtained in many generations, it becomes a partnership not only between those who are living, but between those who are living, those who are dead, and those who are to be born.

Edmund Burke (1729–1797)

Moral Philosophy has two central roles. One is to describe moral reality: to distinguish which values are morally important, to discern how important they are relative to one another . . . in particular circumstances. The other is to guide action. To provide the moral compass which agents need in order to ensure that they act rightly.

Harry Brighouse[1]

INTRODUCTION

Moral growth is an evolutionary process, both for the individual and the society. Democracy requires a certain kind of respect that is different from the expression of respect called for in other settings. Here, an object of respect is the *capacity* of the individual and the society to shape their own development and to determine their own idea of a good life. This calls for an education that aims to promote self-consciousness about existing and emerging possibilities and that enables rising citizens, both as individuals and as part of collective enterprises, to recognize their capacity for growth. Growth involves both therapeutic and creative factors. Therapeutic factors include a capacity to recognize manipulation and to address the distorted aims

---

[1] Harry Brighouse, "Foreword," in Lorella Terzi, ed., *Justice and Equality in Education: A Capacity Perspective on Disability and Special Educational Needs* (London: Continuum, 2008), p. IX.

that it promotes. Creative factors include the ability to realize the value of alternative ideas about the good life and to consider the worth of moral invention in terms of the possibilities available for reducing domination and for advancing moral growth.

DEMOCRATIC RESPECT: THE FIRST AIM OF MORAL EDUCATION

Respect is a foundation of democracy. It is something we owe to each other and something that shapes our institutions and practices. The meaning of respect will differ somewhat depending on whether we refer to political democracy (the rules of governance) or cultural democracy (the shared, tacit understandings that define and facilitate human interaction). On the one hand, the secret ballot is a symbol of political democracy. It is symbolic of the respect given to a voter's independent voice. It signals the norm that a person's vote reflects their own unconditioned, uncoerced judgment, regardless of how they reached that judgment, or barring a bribe, what they took as relevant in doing so. On the other hand, the story of Rosa Parks's refusal to go to the back of the bus is symbolic of cultural democracy, of the idea that everyone deserves equal consideration.

Respect is a foundation of democratic culture when it serves as a recognition of the capacity for individual moral reflection and personal growth. Democratic respect entails the collectively shared assumption that people, regardless of their immediate circumstances, are essentially free beings, capable of informed self-direction and enlightened self-rule. The three-year-old's objection, "You are not the boss of me!" may be taken as the affirmation of a democratic impulse. It is the recognition that, however dependent I may be at this moment, I am ultimately in charge of my own development, and I am deserving of respect. This simple recognition is part of the foundation of cultural democracy, and it belongs to individuals in their own right, rather than to persons as the occupants of social positions, as, say, in a Confucian community or in a rigid class system. As a self-determining person, I have a right to demand respect from you, just as you have a right to demand respect from me. But this does not mean that democracy is an automatic outgrowth of human nature. Human nature creates a possibility, not an inevitability.

A primary aim of moral education then, in a democracy, is to advance the basic idea of democratic respect and the behavior appropriate to it.

DEMOCRATIC RESPECT AND THE EVOLUTION
OF MORAL STANDARDS

Just as individuals can evolve and grow, so too can moral standards within a democratic system. Custodians need to be aware of the evolutionary quality of respect and the possibility for the development of new moral standards. Take, for example, one of the critical concerns of educational feminists – the loss of self-confidence as girls grow into adolescents. The female toddler who argued when she was three "You are not the boss of me!" is observed to become more docile as she grows older.[2] The fact that this loss of self-confidence is *now* an object of concern and research for feminist scholars is a sign of the evolution of moral standards toward gender equality within the self-reinforcing, interlocking norms and justifications that constitute a democratic culture. This evolution is made desirable by both technological innovations, like the substitute of machine for muscles, and cultural changes, such as smaller families, formal schooling, and so on.

This evolution presents two educational tasks for custodians. The immediate task is to connect this evolutionary change to the moral "intuitions" of its rising citizens. If the child is to continue to grow as an agent in her own right, her parents and caretakers need to provide the respect, space, and opportunities that such growth requires. The long-term task is to shape a view of moral education where the evolutionary quality of morality itself is incorporated into

[2] Carol Gilligan, *In a Different Voice: Psychological Theory and Women's Development* (Cambridge: Harvard University Press, 1982), p. 143.

the understanding of democracy. People need to see themselves as capable of self-directed growth through new experiences and rational deliberation, and they need to see existing moral standards as open to change.

AN OPEN MORAL UNIVERSE AS THE PRESUPPOSITION OF DEMOCRATIC RESPECT

Democratic respect as person-related rests on a certain dynamic conception of the moral universe, where moral invention is accepted as a real possibility, and where natality is seen as creating possibilities for moral renewal and transformation. "You are not the boss of me," uttered by a three-year-old in a democratic environment, is likely to merit a very different response than when uttered in an authoritarian household. In the latter, it will likely be viewed as a sign of disrespect, not just of older people, but of a fixed moral order: whereas in the former, it likely will be viewed as a sign of growing independence and as an induction into an open moral universe. The difference represents a different understanding of the moral order; the one, where wisdom is associated with age and gender, and morality is viewed as timeless; the other, where the moral order is adjusted to accommodate innovation and promote growth and novelty. These different conceptions of the moral order themselves are attached to different environmental conditions and different levels of predictability.

The connection between technology and morality suggests that it is not just an individual's moral *understanding* that changes, but the common standards that are used to hold others and ourselves accountable may themselves undergo justifiable change as well. Democratic moral culture, as a loose system of interlocking norms and justifications, will change, often slowly, sometimes rapidly, in response to different environmental conditions and new possibilities. However, to connect moral systems to environmental differences is not to endorse relativism as some cultural anthropologists do. It is simply to acknowledge the need to consider environmental constraints in assessing the appropriateness of different moral systems.

True, judgments of right and wrong are social constructs, but they are not *simply* constructs. In democratic systems, they entail implicit claims about the capacity of normative systems to reduce domination and advancing growth. At any given time, our very best conception of right and wrong, and the behavior that most faithfully conforms to it, may undergo drastic and justifiable change in light of changes in material conditions, technological innovation, or new knowledge.

MORAL INVENTIONS

A democratic moral invention is a conceptual or behavioral innovation that functions to reduce domination, to enable personal growth, and to foster participation. Consider one of the simplest, and most common, moral inventions: shaking hands. Until the Coronavirus (COVID-19), this practice was so common that it is difficult to think of it as an invention, let alone a *moral* invention. Yet some oral traditions trace the handshake back to an ancient world where it served as a sign of peaceful intent, indicating that neither side was threatening with a weapon. If this history is accurate, then the handshake was a monumental moral invention, reducing domination of those with the smaller sword by those with the larger and thus allowing both to go their own way without coercion or domination. As a moral innovation, the handshake reduces threat and increases the possibility of self-determination and growth.

The handshake now has another function in a democracy. It signals the equal status of two parties, regardless of their external circumstances, such as wealth or position. Indeed, the very fact that we refer to these as *external* circumstances is a statement that they are not a part of one's personhood. It assumes that an individual's identity need not be exhausted by one's role. This is one reason why in the COVID epidemic virtual handshakes were still important.

Contrast the handshake as signifying one moral system to the practice of deep, asymmetrical bowing, which signified another.

When someone places himself in a lower position than another person, they indicate vulnerability, trust, and honor. Like the handshake, the bow functions to remove obstacles, but unlike the handshake, it reinforces the idea of a natural hierarchy. Children bow to parents, wives bow to husbands, daughters-in-law bow to mothers-in-law, workers bow to bosses, and owners of smaller companies bow lower and sooner than do owners of larger ones. Just as we might imagine two knights of old baring their hands and allowing the one to grasp and inspect the other, so too might we imagine the commoner lowering his head in front of the samurai's sword to display his absolute trust. The history of the handshake also suggests trust, but of a different kind – trust but verify – that presupposes a relation among equals where both have the authority to verify.[3]

The handshake is no longer thought of as a major moral invention because the conditions that it was intended to address are no longer relevant in the same way. Still, if you ever had your extended hand ignored, the slight that you feel may be related to the fear that some distant ancestor felt when a sword unexpectedly greeted his extended hand.

Moral education for cultural democracy then involves, in part, teaching students to recognize and consider new moral inventions as responses to new conditions. The larger goal is not just to teach students a certain behavioral custom – this is how you shake hands – although this may be a first step. It is to help them understand how behavioral customs develop as moral inventions in response to changing conditions and in relation to the interconnected norms of moral paradigms.

APPRAISING MORAL INVENTIONS

The worth of democratic moral inventions is appraised by their capacity to reduce domination and take advantage of new possibilities

---

[3] Walter Feinberg, *Japan and the Pursuit of a New American Identity* (New York: Routledge, 1993).

often made viable by new knowledge and technological changes. Consider, for example, the birth-control pill as a technological innovation. It not only allowed women to control childbirth but also created conditions for new moral inventions. As mentioned in an earlier chapter, among these was an addition to the English language: the title *Ms.* as an alternative to either *Mrs.* or *Miss.* This was not just a change in titles. It involved the replacement of one moral system, where women and men complemented each other in their separate spheres, by another in which women and men deserve equal consideration in any sphere, from the home to the military to outer space.

And with this change came a brand-new vocabulary. Terms such as "glass ceiling," "sexual harassment," "sex discrimination," and "marital rape" were added to the English lexicon. Ideas about fairness and unfairness continue to undergo change as a part of the wider shift in the culture of democracy. Children who do not learn how to identify this change will be left behind, confused, and bewildered. Yet children who only learn to follow these changes without understanding why they were made, or the changes in the moral norms they entail, will be almost as disadvantaged as those who insist on resisting them. They will find themselves subject to future shifts in judgment and allegiance, which they may tend to resist, viewing them as immoral rather than as possibly rational responses to changing conditions. When we understand the reason for a rule – the function it serves – we are better able to adjust behavior to changing conditions. These changes of course create new problems, and the need for deeper understanding and more careful research, as is the case today with the possibility of medical treatment for "gender dysphoria" and the great cost of mistakes – in either direction.

MORALLY OPEN UNIVERSE AS A CONDITION FOR DEMOCRACY

The argument for a morally open universe as a condition for democracy is twofold. First, moral inventions are real, and any particular invention is at some point in time a novelty. Before the invention of the handshake, perhaps the moral thing to do would have been to submit yourself to the strongest warlord as a way to save your family. Where the possibility of moral invention exists, so does the possibility of moral progress. Second, democratic agency requires that people *believe* that they can make a difference in creating the conditions for and conceiving of a new and different moral order. Today the environmental movement and the conception of nature that is emerging from it are examples of the importance of moral innovation.

Moral inventions are often the cause for struggles before they are adopted. Often this is because of the deeper conflict between competing moral paradigms. To return to an earlier example, the addition of the innovative title *Ms.* fit with other changes that were already under way. As previously mentioned, new techniques to control the timing of birth provided a technological change that helped to make certain positions available to women as equal to men (as long as the law cooperates). The designated titles *Mrs.* and *Miss* had served as signs that a woman was less than fully committed to her work outside the home. Opposition to the adoption of the title *Ms.* was often taken as an indication of a person who believed that family was the appropriate sphere for a woman and that *Mrs.* was the telos for any *Miss.* *Ms.* was a significant moral invention because it signaled women need not have any different commitment to the work world than men and that there was an alternative to every *Miss* becoming a *Mrs.* But before it was accepted, many people, maintaining the traditional idea of woman's work, treated the title *Ms.* as an aberration, or dismissed it as just another example of meaningless obnoxious political correctness. Yet it is more than interesting that, since the wide-scale adoption of *Ms.*, a formerly common term – *spinster* – has largely gone out of use, indicating that there is nothing *remarkable* about a woman without a man.

Not all moral inventions are widely adopted, and many struggle to gain acceptance. However, the closer the connection that a new struggling innovation can claim to an older established one, the greater may be its chance for success. Consider this objection to the proposed pronoun innovation "they is," which was published in *The New York Times* a few years ago.

> The last major linguistic innovation we English speakers underwent in response to social change was the spread of "Ms." In the 1970's. This allowed half the population to choose not to identify themselves by marital status. The universal use of the singular "they," by contrast, would compel all speakers to change virtually every sentence in deference to the half percent of the population who identify as nonbinary.
>
> In the process, it would destroy ancient and universal linguistic distinctions of gender, and, much worse, the distinction between the singular and the plural, which is essential to linguistic clarity.
>
> For most of us gender remains a fundamental and uncontroversial aspect of how we identify ourselves and one another. The male and female genders are conceived more broadly and fluidly today than ever before. Those who nonetheless identify with neither gender are entitled to their freedom of identity and expression, and to our respect.
>
> But that obligation of respect does not include an obligation to recast our language, and the expectation of this accommodation should not become the next liberal litmus test by which non-adopters will be shames and ostracized.
>
> We can support the rights of gender minorities without upending our language.[4]

Yet the author neglects to consider that the singular *they* shares much with the earlier *Ms*. They are both tied to a web of conceptual innovations. Many grammarian purists had as much concern about shifting from the universal masculine *he* and *his* to the gender neutral *he/she*. The aim of these inventions is to de-normalize certain ways of being, and to open up space for new ways of thinking about what to count as normal.

---

[4] Ron Meyers, "Letter to the Editor," *The New York Times*, July 18, 2019, p. A24.

What I am interested in here is not debating the merits of the linguistic innovation *they is*, but rather to use the proposed locution as an example of the way a moral innovation occurs and the struggles to accept it. Clearly a linguistic shift that includes a conventional plural pronoun, like *they*, with a conventionally singular verb, like *is*, can be jarring, and if preserving linguistic convention was the only thing at stake, the victory would go to the grammatical conservative. But that is not the only thing at stake.

THE ROLE OF KNOWLEDGE IN MORAL INNOVATION

The resistance to the use of *Ms.* indicates that the contest over *they is*, is wider than a grammatical duel between pronouns, and that grammar is not fixed once and for all. It is subject to new understandings and new knowledge. We can, for example, track rates of depression and suicide among gender dysphoria suffering people, especially children and teens.[5] So we know there is a steep cost that many pay for living in a society where they cannot fit into the most basic categories of identity.

Granted, this knowledge by itself has not always been sufficient to carry the day. Until recently both religious leaders and psychiatrists looked upon what some labeled as "gender confusion," especially when related to homosexuality, as a moral failure of the individual, and suicide was seen as evidence, not of the restrictiveness of the categories, but as an individual moral or spiritual failure. And so, for these people, the failure to fit into established sexual categories did not call for a social change; it called for an individual, therapeutic, or spiritual one. Those who demand a shift in the grammatical landscape are both implicitly and explicitly challenging this traditional way of understanding the individual distress that accompanies sexual ambiguity.

---

[5] García-Vega et al., "Suicide Ideation and Suicide Attempts in Persons with Gender Dysphoria" (National Library of Medicine, National Center for Biotechnical Information, August 30, 2018) PubMed.gov.

At the deepest level, the challenge is to the very idea that there is anything really ambiguous or dysphoric about affirming an alternative sexual identity, whether that identity be the physical attraction to members of the same sex or a strong desire to change one's sex from male to female or female to male. Change is likely coming as a result of many interlocking factors. Among them are an increasing knowledge about the biology of sexuality, feminist and queer scholarship that disassociates the concept of sex from the concept of gender, and literary works that sympathetically bring us into the life experience of sexually unconventional individuals.[6]

THE LIMITS OF MORAL ABSOLUTISM AND MORAL FLUIDITY

Moral absolutism is the doctrine that moral principles do not change, and moral action is the same at all times and in all places. Those who hold this doctrine are often skeptical of democracy because it is messy, allowing everyone to select the rulers and anyone, so selected, to rule. Instead, absolutists favor leadership by the "morally best," the "aristos," whether selected by religious tradition, heroic action, or other methods.

Although absolutism allows that given greater maturity, our moral *understanding* may grow, it rejects the possibility that true moral ideals change. Take Plato and his allegory of the Cave as an example. For Plato, while people can come closer and closer to the good, and hence grow in their own individual knowledge, the idea of the good does not change. It is what it is. If something is morally good at Time 1 and Place 2, it will also be morally good at Time x and Place y. In other words, the absolutist allows that individual moral growth is possible but not the potential growth of the moral order itself. This is viewed as fixed, regardless of whether or not particular individuals recognize it.

Absolutism is often cited as a justification for authoritarian practices, whether in the home (e.g., father knows best; children

---

[6] Jeffrey Eugenides, *Middlesex* (New York: Farrar, Straus and Giroux, 2002).

should be seen but not heard) or the doctor's office (e.g., the doctor knows best) or in the halls of power (e.g., philosophers should be kings). However, some believe that absolutism is consistent with certain forms of democracy, especially with the belief that discussion and debate can guide us to the morally right action. Given this view, our *knowledge* of the good may undergo change, but morality, akin to Plato's idea of the good, itself does not.

LIMITS OF MORAL ABSOLUTISM

Absolutism is an inadequate understanding of either democracy or morality because it does not consider the changes in material conditions and technology that drive moral struggle and innovation. Nor does it allow for moral evolution as a response to changing needs, new knowledge, or changing material conditions and technology.

A more adequate conception of democracy allows that the evolution of the individual and the moral order can go together. New knowledge makes a difference in the moral order, just as new conditions change the contingencies that must be accommodated. This, more fluid conception of democracy, promotes a more dialogical conception of moral understanding, one where the elements of both the past and the emerging moral order become relevant for understanding moral conflict and shaping moral change.

The fluid conception of democracy promotes a more relative status of morality. However, the relativism here is not one where anything goes or where every individual is the absolute arbiter of what is right and wrong. Morality is relative in the sense that it can develop and grow, and it is also relative to the context in which moral action is called for. For democracy, the growth is measured not by any absolute standard but in terms of the primary idea of cultural democracy that includes the reduction of domination for the sake of growth. If there is an absolute standard, it must be a formal one, such as nondomination. The substance of that definition will change as a result of changing possibilities brought by changes in social, environmental, or technological conditions. Moral education involves sensitizing students to an awareness of these changes and developing the capacity to respond appropriately to the possibilities they present.

MORAL EVOLUTION IS CONSISTENT WITH
DEMOCRATIC IDEALS

The tension between the absolutist and the relativist conceptions of democracy is a piece of American history. The Declaration of Independence reflects both. Whereas Jefferson's "inalienable rights" suggests absolutism, the US Constitution's grammatically problematic phrase, "In order to establish a *more* perfect union," suggests the possibility of a certain kind of moral growth, one where one stage of perfection becomes the platform through which future needs are identified and future stages of perfection are glimpsed. It also suggests the scaffold through which new forms of morality are developed.

The phrase *"a more perfect union"* suggests that perfection itself, and not just our ideas of perfection, change. Given the right circumstances, it can grow. (This incidentally is one reason why an originalist interpretation of the Constitution is an oxymoron. To read the Constitution in terms of some fixed intent contradicts the very spirit in which the Constitution was written.) Moral (not just moral knowledge) growth is a critical tenet of cultural democracy, and it requires a different kind of understanding of the quality of moral judgment, and a different kind of character. "A more perfect union" suggests that, in hindsight, many of our existing ideas of right and wrong will become outmoded, as conditions change and new possibilities come into view. But these changing conditions bring more than new knowledge – they also bring new moral possibilities.

Moral progress is possible for the same reason that other kinds of progress are possible. Changing conditions allow for new developments and new inventions – technological, conceptual, and moral – and, most importantly, new ends. As Dewey wrote:

> Progress is sometimes thought of as consisting in getting nearer to
> ends already sought. But this is a minor form of progress, for it

requires only improvement of the means of action or technical advance. More important modes of progress consist in enriching prior purposes and in forming new ones. Desires are not a fixed quantity, nor does progress mean only an increased amount of satisfaction. With increased culture and new mastery of nature, new desires, demands for new qualities of satisfaction, show themselves, for intelligence perceives new possibilities of action.[7]

Some new inventions largely provide, in Dewey's terms, more effective means to reach already well-defined goals. Take the self-driving car. Its successful development will depend on innovations in camera technology, new sensors, computers, and guidance systems, among other things, but for the most part it will not change our desired destinations. They remain the same. In contrast, imagine the invention of conceptual innovation, such as the directional coordinates – north, east, south, and west – and the tremendous impact this invention has had on desire formation. Here, there is a continuing interaction between the invention and the desires that they made possible, enabling people to imagine new and distant places and to then travel to them. Where once it might have been sufficient to describe the local landscape to a traveler – go to the river, look for the hill, follow the path, and so on – the invention of the compass and more stable boats made long-distance travel safer and more predictable, and likely this in turn enabled new possibilities to be imagined and new desires to be formed. But the coordinates are conceptual. They indicate no real place. Keep traveling toward the west from California and you wind up in the Far East.[8]

As with technical and conceptual progress, moral progress is tied to the openings shaped by innovations and their implications for reformulated desire. For democratic moral education, the direction of progress is toward greater inclusion and respect. Given time and

---

[7] John Dewey, *Democracy and Education* (New York: Macmillan, 1916), pp. 223–224.
[8] At least according to those who go by the Colonial invention of Greenwich (England) Mean Time. Appreciation to Daniel Brudney for this observation.

innovation, the content and methods of moral education may undergo changes that allow for new desires to take shape.

Take the changing Catholic ban on usury as an example of a moral innovation. The Church's original prohibition of lending money for interest is now interpreted as a rejection of human exploitation, of which lending money for interest may or may not be a case.[9] In order to understand the change, we might put ourselves in the position of a member of a small, stable Middle Age peasant community that depended on maintaining peaceful face-to-face relationships – much like those in a family. One of the fastest ways to create discord in a family or a tight-knit community is to use another family member's or a neighbor's misery to your own advantage. In such a community, if your brother needs money to save his house or a neighbor needs money to save the crop, you are expected to lend it without requesting interest.

The restrictions on usury, as protection against destructive discord, was a very practical matter, with profound moral implications. This is likely one reason that money lending was often relegated to Jews, the perennial outsiders. It is more than accidental that once borrowing became critical for new ventures and for the growth of capital, the definition of usury began to change. Today, as mentioned earlier, the Church uses the term "usury," not to indicate the lending of money for interest but to describe the sinful exploitation of one human being by another. Altering the meaning of usury enabled a widening of the community to include Protestants and, eventually even Jews, as well as other people, and this move toward greater inclusion reflected progress both in the individual and in the moral order.

To recognize the reality of moral innovation and the fact that morality may change as a justified response to changing conditions and new knowledge does not mean that anything goes. There is often a family of core ideas that ties the old moral order to the new. The

---

[9] The Catechism of the Catholic Church (Saint Paul, MN; Wanderer, 1994).

case of usury serves as an example. Maintaining community solidarity required not exploiting members of your family or your immediate community, and in time, the principle of nonexploitation was extended by Catholics to fellow Catholics, their coreligionists. The modern restriction has simply extended that principle beyond the confines of one religion. Lending money for interest is no longer equated with exploitation unless the interest is excessive. It may well result in a mutual gain. The moral order changes as new needs and new possibilities arise. Yet our understanding of the moral order rests on broader organizing principles, such as "do not exploit other people," even as the idea of exploitation may change. Still, democratic moral education requires that rising citizens have an understanding of the history of specific moral changes, as well as opportunities to identify in the future unresolved contemporary moral issues.

SHAPING OUR MORAL BOUNDARIES

> Vice, for vice is necessary to be shewn, should always disgust; nor should the grace of gaiety, or the dignity of courage, be so united with it, as to reconcile it to the mind. Wherever it appears, it should raise hatred by the malignity of its practices, and contempt by the meanness of its stratagems; for while it is supported by either parts or spirit, it will be seldom heartily abhorred.[10]

> Samuel Johnson

A great deal of our moral behavior is necessarily incorporated into our instinctive responses. It would be greatly inefficient, even threatening, if we had to think though the correct response for every immediate situation. Much of what we believe is learned through reinforcement. As moralists like Samuel Johnson warned (in the previous quote), mixed messages can be dangerous. Let vice be exposed as vice; do not couple it with a virtue. Today, some see conscience formation as a potential subsection of the biological sciences, and some expect that brain-imaging may eventually show the role that

---

[10] Samuel Johnson in Ramler No. 4, quoted by William Ian Miller, *The Anatomy of Disgust* (Cambridge: Harvard University Press, 1997), p. 179.

the frontal cortex and other parts of the brain, such as the amygdala, play in the formation of conscience.[11] Still, moral development requires more than just a clear message reinforced positively or negatively, or a well-massaged amygdala.

Whatever the mechanism of moral development may be, it is critical that it be attached to morally appropriate objects, as we best understand them, and in a morally appropriate and historically sensitive way. And while the shaping of moral instincts is a necessary part of moral education, democratic moral education requires the capacity to become aware of the appropriateness of habitual responses to a given situation. One does not need to be a Freudian to recognize that we may come to misrecognize certain situations according to some earlier experience and then, because of that misrecognition, respond inappropriately to new situations.

WHY SEPARATE MORALITY FROM MORAL KNOWLEDGE

Morality has an objective pole. It is estimated by the actual reduction in domination and in the conditions for growth that are made available at any given time. Different times will present different conditions for reduction in domination and for growth, and these must be considered in making fair judgment about the actual moral situation in any one time or place. Moral knowledge has to do with the level of understanding that people have of these possibilities. Even Jefferson began to question his own racism when confronted with the brilliant mathematical work of Benjamin Banneker, a Black man. Writing to the French mathematician, de Condorcet, Jefferson began to change his views on the inherent inferiority of Black people:

> I am happy to inform you that we have now in the United States a negro, the son of a black man born in Africa, and a black woman born in the United States, who is a very respectable mathematician. . . . I have seen very elegant solutions of

---

[11] See Patricia S. Churchill, *Conscience: The Origins of Moral Intuition* (New York: W. W. Norton, 2019).

Geometrical problems by him. Add to this that he is a very worthy & respectable member of society. He is a free man. I shall be delighted to see these instances of moral eminence so multiplied as to prove that the want of talent observed in them is merely the effect of their degraded condition, and not proceeding from any difference in the structure of the parts on which intellect depends.[12]

Sadly, of the 600 people Jefferson enslaved, he freed only 10. While Jefferson refused to free most of his slaves, his response to Banneker can serve to demonstrate how new information can begin to pry open otherwise closed moral judgments.

CONCLUSION

Democracy is a moral practice and democratic citizenship is both a moral standing and a practical vocation. A person with the standing of citizen has certain political and civil rights, such as equal protection *under the law*, the right to vote, and so forth. While individuals are *born* or *granted standing* as citizen, citizenship as a *vocation* is something that is *chosen*, and that has practical collective benefits. It provides feedback mechanisms that serve to forecast and minimize harm; it promotes wide-scale participation, encouraging others to see themselves as active stakeholders in joint projects, and it stimulates useful innovation. Democracy as a practical activity may be especially useful in situations of environmental uncertainty and social upheaval when "tried and true" methods can no longer be counted on to work. In these circumstances, informed democratic participation serves to channel competing ideas into cooperative responses by engaging different interests and perspectives, by controlling uncertainty, by reducing undesirable side effects, and by taking advantage of underdeveloped opportunities. Democratic participation changes people. It changes their interests, aims, and habits. It changes their characteristic ways of behaving (i.e., their characters).

[12] Quoted in Michael Meyerson, *We the People: Political Numeracy* (New York: W. W. Norton, 2002), p. 131.

The moral order in a democracy consists of both relatively stable and unstable elements, but what will count as stable and unstable is often recognized only in hindsight. Because change is a condition of democracy, it is not sufficient to just teach how to behave to conform to an existing social order. It is also critical to teach how to think about right and wrong in new and unanticipated situations, and for a belief in the possibility of renewal.

> When day comes we ask ourselves,
> where can we find light in this never-ending shade?
> The loss we carry,
> a sea we must wade
> We've braved the belly of the beast
> We've learned that quiet isn't always peace
> And the norms and notions
> of what just is
> Isn't always just-ice
> And yet the dawn is ours
> before we knew it
> Somehow, we do it
> Somehow, we've weathered and witnessed
> a nation that isn't broken
> but simply unfinished.[13]
>
> Amanda Gorman, "The Hill We Climb"

[13] Amanda Gorman, "The Hill We Climb." Presidential Inaugural Poem, January 20, 2021. www.cnbc.com/2021/01/20/amanda-gormans-inaugural-poem-the-hill-we-climb-full-text.html.

Index

Printed in the USA
CPSIA information can be obtained
at www.ICGtesting.com
LVHW090024231023
761811LV00004BA/421